Cyber Intelligence-Driven Risk

Cyber Intelligence-Driven Risk

How to Build and Use Cyber Intelligence for Business Risk Decisions

RICHARD O. MOORE III,
MSIA, CISSP, CISM

WILEY

Published by John Wiley & Sons, Inc., Hoboken, New Jersey.
Published simultaneously in Canada.

For general information on our other products and services or for technical support, please contact our Customer Care Department within the United States at (800) 762-2974, outside the United States at (317) 572-3993, or fax (317) 572-4002.

Wiley publishes in a variety of print and electronic formats and by print-on-demand. Some material included with standard print versions of this book may not be included in e-books or in print-on-demand. If this book refers to media such as a CD or DVD that is not included in the version you purchased, you may download this material at http://booksupport.wiley.com . For more information about Wiley products, visit www .wiley.com.

Library of Congress Cataloging-in-Publication Data

Names: Moore, Richard O., III, 1971- author.
Title: Cyber intelligence-driven risk : how to build and use cyber
   intelligence for business risk decisions / by Richard O. Moore III,
   MSIA, CISSP, CISM.
Description: Hoboken, New Jersey : John Wiley & Sons, [2021] | Includes
   bibliographical references and index.
Identifiers: LCCN 2020035540 (print) | LCCN 2020035541 (ebook) | ISBN
   9781119676843 (cloth) | ISBN 9781119676911 (adobe pdf) | ISBN
   9781119676898 (epub)
Subjects: LCSH: Business enterprises—Security measures. | Data protection.
   | Cyber intelligence (Computer security) | Risk management.
Classification: LCC HD61.5 .M66 2021 (print) | LCC HD61.5 (ebook) | DDC
   658.15/5–dc23
LC record available at https://lccn.loc.gov/2020035540
LC ebook record available at https://lccn.loc.gov/2020035541

Cover Design: Wiley
Cover Image: © whiteMocca/Getty Images

Contents

Preface

Knowing is different from doing, and therefore theory must never be used as norms for a standard, but merely as aids to judgment.

– Carl von Clausewitz

OVER THE past decade, organizations have continued to acquire technologies and monitoring systems, and have focused technology personnel only on protecting the organization's external perimeters and forgetting simple cyber hygiene. What is missing from many organizations is how cyber intelligence knowledge is leveraged to enhance business risk decision-making processes. This book is a body of work that is consistently evolving to meet new cyber risks, address the lack of cyber-skilled individuals, and provide more efficient processes to enhance the cyber defensive posture of an organization. The CI-DR™ program we will be discussing here is about building or enhancing an "intelligence capability" (i.e. cyber) that is traditionally missing during risk management conversations and business strategies. Where business risk management is a common practice, the cyber intelligence component is emergent in how operational risk can discuss the velocity and impact to business risk management and provide a distinctive outcome regarding strategy. We believe that building the connective tissues of cyber intelligence and business risk management by outlining capabilities and functions into a cohesive program creates significant business value. We call that collection the Cyber Intelligence–Driven Risk (CI-DR™) methodology.

CI-DR is a proven methodology in building cyber programs, as it not only defines the connectivity between functions and capabilities but creates a different view of how cyber information is used, and improves the business risk processes that plague many organizations. The CI-DR program methodology is essential to any sized organization looking to build, enhance, understand, and grow their cyber defensive capabilities and cyber operational risk programs. The CI-DR program framework can provide guidance and direction that will mitigate consistent failures to respond and react appropriately to emerging cyber risks. The CI-DR methodology is designed to provide business leaders with clear information to make decisions and understand the impact a cyber incident can have on the business. A CI-DR program is very different from the traditional application of cyber threat intelligence, which is a subcomponent where technical details are passed from a managed security service provider (MSSP) or a security operations center (SOC) and are used by internal leaders of technology or cybersecurity. A CI-DR program enhances the traditional approach of intelligence, cybersecurity, and risk management by using a collaborative fused program consisting of dedicated intelligence analysts from both the business and cybersecurity disciplines who can turn information into a business risk decision.

CI-DR does not change how traditional business intelligence (BI) operates but provides a framework for cyber intelligence enhancements that benefits current BI functions and provides the intersection with operational risk management. Having each of these capabilities operating as part of the connective tissue ecosystem enhances business decision structures. Terms such as "risk intelligence," "network intelligence," and "cyber threat intelligence" have been around since 2008. However, these concepts have not been consistently implemented to harness and leverage the information required for today's business decisions. Excluding some of the Fortune 100 companies, many have done little to adopt cybersecurity risks or cyber intelligence "knowledge" into their business risk management objectives. Those companies continue to focus the majority of budgets on purchasing new technology to try and enhance their security posture, but are consistently finding failure in that process.

This book references and is built on military intelligence lessons learned and processes that have been proven by best practices used for giving military commanders the ability to understand their area of operations and key strategic objectives. The CI-DR program leverages these key concepts and adopts them for business leaders to enhance their business operational risk objectives. This is the first book of a series designed for visionary cyber professionals striving to develop and improve outdated cyber defense systems and design a future-proof cyber program that contributes to enhanced business risk decision-making. This initial book provides the foundations for the creation of an actionable (i.e. build and use) CI-DR program that can be applied tomorrow to solve the gap between enterprise risk management, security architecture, and the current management of cyber risks in use today. Additionally, this book leaves out specific vendor technology solutions, as we want to focus the reader on how cyber intelligence functions and capabilities can drive better risk decision structures in today's digital age. By mentioning technology solutions we mask the foundational cyber concepts needed to drive decisions to keep up with the velocity of business changes. Additionally, this book can be used by cybersecurity professionals, software architects, mergers-and-acquisitions teams, government "think tanks," academics, and students looking to help businesses make better choices about risk by building a proper program focused on delivering risk options to the decision-maker.

NOTES

Every industry can benefit by creating or enhancing their business risk management program. Our CI-DR framework provides you, the reader, with the opportunity to build these capabilities, whether internally built, acquired through merger or acquisition, or sourced from the many service providers; this handbook provides the tools and the framework needed to ensure that it is effective. By the end of this book, the reader should understand what functional capabilities are needed to build a CI-DR program; the importance of why the "connective tissue" between the functions and capabilities is so valuable, and how the CI-DR program can be adequately leveraged to assist leaders in making more informed business decisions in the era of increased emergent cyber threats and attacks. Depending on the level of business understanding, the reader will be able to:

- Build, buy, or outsource certain functions of the cyber intelligence–driven risk program.
- Understand the functional capabilities needed to have an active program.
- Turn cyber intelligence "knowledge" into business risk decisions.
- Effectively use cyber intelligence to support enterprise and operational risk management programs.
- Reduce the impact of cyber events through cyber intelligence "knowledge" for many business operations and not just through purchasing of new technologies.

- Leverage a cyber intelligence–driven risk program to support mergers and acquisitions and collect the benefits of predictive cyber intelligence analytics.
- Understand how the CI-DR program can reduce loss from cyber events for the organization and provide a proactive cyber defensive posture needed to meet emerging threats.

If this book inspires you to create new technologies, build a company to support these capabilities, or reduce risk and costs to your organization, please drop us a note on social media (@cybersixactual) or send us an email (https://www.cybersix.com), we would love to hear from you.

Acknowledgments

AS WE come out of the 2020 pandemic, many of us give pause to think about who we are, where we came from, and where we are going. This book would not be possible to complete and keep consistent without the assistance and support of colleagues, students, friends, and contributing authors. I would like to thank the United States Marine Corps for giving me drive, direction, skills, and a brotherhood that has been forged by combat. I would also like to thank SPAWAR (now NAVWAR) for giving me the information security skills to make my career possible. To Norwich University's Graduate MSIA program for providing an education second to none. To Northeastern University and Salve Regina University for providing me the opportunity to give back to the information security community and educate the next generation of cybersecurity professionals. I also want to thank those who supported my career growth and provided mentorship throughout my years in the cybersecurity profession. My first mentor and first Chief Information Security Officer (CISO), John Schramm, who was at the time leading the Investor's Bank and Trust Information Security group. John, as a prior US Army Officer, led me to take a position in KPMG's Information Protection group in lieu of rejoining the US government. My second mentor and the CISO who challenged me to succeed is Jim Routh. Jim was the first CISO I worked for who had transformational programs and business objectives tied to moving cyber activities into the forefront of business decisions. My last CISO, who mentored me in patience and helped develop my transformational concepts, is Steve Attias. Steve had been a CISO at New York Life since the declaration of that industry title, and continues to advise companies on cybersecurity programs in his retirement. Finally, to my mentor-friend, Marc Sokol. Marc was the Chief Security Officer at Guardian Life when I was at New York Life but had a good decade of experience in leading an insurance company's cybersecurity programs. Marc was instrumental in my growth, executive experiences, and still assists today where I need additional help or support.

To the contributing authors, my colleagues, and friends, you all have been a part of my journey in building these programs, listened to my ideas and concepts over social gatherings, working hours, and late-night meetups. Without your direct feedback, opinions, and execution, I would have never been able to see these programs work firsthand. We have built these programs in two Fortune 100 companies to great success, and many of you are still working on those programs or have modified them to support your current environments.

There were many throughout my career who have been a part of building out these concepts into reality and there were people who gave me the support and freedom to build these programs. I would like to directly name and thank the following individuals who had a direct impact in helping to build and refine many of my concepts into programs over the last two decades. From my time at KPMG I wish to thank Neil Bryden, Barbara Cousins, Greig Arnold, and Prasad Shenoy; it was the time when the CI-DR™ concepts began to originate. I wish to thank those individuals at the Royal Bank of Scotland, Americas, who instituted and implemented the first of the CI-DR program's capabilities: Dr. Stephen Johnson (one of the co-authors of this book), Todd Hammond, David Griffeth, Chuck Thomas, Steven Savard, Robert Fitz, James McCoy, Chris Piacitelli, Frank Susi, Jack Atoyan, and David Najac. I wish to thank those responsible for implementing CI-DR version two of capabilities and functions at New York Life: Dr. Stephen Johnson, Robert Sasson, Karen Riha, Eric Grossman, Willard Dawson, and Lee Ramos. Finally, I wish the thank the following individuals at Alvarez and Marsal for creating the documentation behind these programs and putting to paper standard operating procedures, guides for building, and guides for assessing the maturity of these programs: Derek Olson (one of the co-authors of this book), Adele Merritt, Tom Stamulis, Brady Willis, Joe Nemec, Terence Goggins, Dominic Richmond, and Cassidy Lynch.

To my students and those asking me to be their mentors, thank you for listening to my rantings and ravings about our profession. You challenge me daily to be operational, effective, and creative about transformational solutions to meet the demands of the profession and industries you all strive to protect.

To my CyberSix advisors, specifically Sean Cross, who not only has looked out for the best interest of the company but has become a great friend, business partner, mentor, and coach. Your friendship and advice are what all startup organizations need to succeed from running the Founders' Roundtable, bringing startup CEOs to learn from each other, to the exhaustive time and effort you put into all those who need your services. To Steve Dufour, thank you for your strategic guidance and help in solidifying my concepts into business plans and paving the way for future services for my company. I look forward to continuing partnering, collaborating, and working together.

To my dad, whom we lost during the pandemic in 2020, due to underlying conditions. His passing placed a long pause on completing this book.

Finally, to my wife, Jennifer, who encouraged me to pursue this cyber-security profession against many objections, before this profession became so popular. Those years of having to live above a garage raising our children while attending my undergraduate degree and continued service in the U.S. Marine Corps Reserve, through working full-time and completing my graduate degree, to becoming a professor and then moving the family for unknown adventures in this cyberworld; it could not be done without your continued support and love.

Introduction

It is even better to act quickly and err than to hesitate until the time of action is past.

– Carl von Clausewitz

THIS BOOK is designed for business leaders who are looking to unwrap the "cyber black box" and understand how cyber intelligence can improve their business decisions. For the cybersecurity professional who is trying to find an entry point to provide value to executives, and for the cybersecurity teams looking to raise their level of sophistication, this book will address the fundamental issues facing businesses and individuals today. First, organizations are still failing to respond to cyber threats due to inconsistent decisions and poor cyber hygiene. Second, both organizations and cybersecurity professionals are struggling with compliance frameworks, international legislation, and local legislative and other privacy requirements while still trying to make revenue through technology advantages. All of the frameworks, compliance, and privacy items are focused on the technology and not on how the organization should be looking at operational risk. By the end of this book, we will explain to the reader why the CI-DR™ is the center of gravity for decisions that business leaders should be taking advantage of. Business leaders in every organization are consistently being asked how the organization is dealing with cybersecurity issues, whether it can respond to cyber losses, and what the shareholders need to know should a cybersecurity breach or cyber loss leading to financial consequences occur. Most of the cybersecurity issues that current business models outline are reactive in nature and are usually actioned without much analysis or debate, leaving biased opinions and hasty approaches that ultimately detract from logical decisions.

Operational risk losses or consequences are defined in the IEC/ISO 31010[1] documentation and is where we begin to leverage the language needed to bring the CI-DR "knowledge" to the risk management professionals. To have a seat at the table as cyber professionals we need to be able to speak the same taxonomy as our business risk managers. Throughout the book we provide some real-world examples of how a CI-DR program assisted organizations where these capabilities were implemented and matured to assist in the business decision-making process. As you read the examples, our intent is to have you think about the role you hold at your company, or your next role, and the types of information you would want to assist you in making decisions. To be successful, it is key to have the data and knowledge, coupled with curiosity and the desire to be of value that will ultimately lead to being granted access to the internal decision-making for your organization.

With every chapter we provide the business need for a CI-DR program with a real-world example of the cybersecurity issues that many organizations have faced in the past. As you may recall, the year 2012 was very troubling for the financial services, banking, and cybersecurity practitioners. Starting in the month of September and continuing into the new year, a sympathetic nation-state of malicious actors known as QCF (Cyber Fighters of Izz ad-Din al Qassam, also known as Qassam Cyber Fighters) began to methodically stop banks from financially transacting with customers, through an attack known as a Distributed Denial of Service (DDoS). This is essentially a technical mechanism that consumes and overwhelms systems and networks, rendering them unavailable or useless for the purposes they were designed for. Many of these banking institutions leveraged their membership in the Financial Services Information Sharing and Analysis Center (FS-ISAC)[2] to gain an understanding of how the attack started and to provide a secure forum for discussing best strategies to defend the banks against this adversary, helping to set the foundations for many cyber programs and processes in use today.

The ISAC provided the necessary connections among cybersecurity professionals, many of whom came from the military intelligence profession, with a forum and location to share threat intelligence as well as the ability to discuss new capabilities and mitigation process to reduce the attacks against their financial institutions without retribution for competitive interests.

---

[1] International Electrotechnical Commission, Risk Management – Risk Management Techniques, 2009–2011, www.iec.ch/searchpub
[2] Financial Services – Information Sharing and Analysis Center, 1999, located on the internet at https://www.fsisac.com/who-we-are

The Security and Exchange Commission later issued a statement that cyber-security and threat intelligence cannot be a competitive advantage.[3] The larger member institutions had begun building cyber intelligence programs and sharing information on attacks through the membership's cyber intelligence leaders. As executives continued to hear through headlines and peers throughout the banking community, their concerns were how much money they would need to spend to protect their organizations and whether they had the proper staffing and expertise on hand to do that. The action and outcomes of this specific attack played a significant role in the development of the CI-DR program. One of the important processes that was implemented from the sharing of information through the ISAC was the need for cyber intelligence teams to collect, analyze, and produce reporting of attack vectors to the banking management teams for decisions on how to deploy resources.

At different phases of the attack other institutions were doing similar activities, and after months of analysis and the velocity and growth of the attacks, teams using the initial vision of the CI-DR program were able to create a predictive analysis when the attack might occur. Most conversations that were happening in business leadership were not the old similar technology mitigation discussions; the conversations quickly changed focus to discuss whether this attack would impact capital reserves, what other risks might be encountered during this unprecedented cyberattack, and what amount of financial transactions and revenue losses would online banking systems and internet-facing systems incur. As these conversations grew and expanded, our organization had a plan to have the accountants and business analysts review the systems and provide transactional and revenue estimations for eight, sixteen, and twenty-four hours to determine the amount of loss each critical system could incur. Much of this information was derived from work done by the risk management team during their Business Impact Analysis reviews, and the "crown jewels" asset risk assessments conducted by the information security and business technology teams. One of the most difficult assessments that the accountants had to deal with was figuring out potential revenue loss and the number of hours it would take to lose it. This process that was incorporated after the attacks subsided is the original iteration of what is commonly called today a fusion center. A CI-DR fusion center can exist when bringing business owners, accountants, technologists, risk managers, cyber intelligence analysts, and cybersecurity personnel together to solve an organizational problem.

---

[3] SEC memo

Having generated all available intelligence through the fusion of stake-holders, combined with our analysis of all data brought from the fusion teams, a decision model was presented to the Board of Directors for their agreement that we were doing the right thing. That "knowledge" package painted key cyber intelligence decision points and pinpointed that the organization would be attacked somewhere around January 7 at 14:00, and that the financial loss would be over a million dollars for eight hours of outage time. Additionally, the decision points included mitigation technologies the organization could deploy to remediate the attack and the cost comparison against the impact of loss. The cost-benefit decision weighed with risk options provided two courses of recommended actions. The decision points were to either allow our systems to be overwhelmed and let the attackers think they took us offline, or implement this new unproven Anti-DDoS scrubbing technology, which could still potentially lose some real transactions with an additional cost for ineffective technology. With agreement that executive management had the situation well understood, the decision was made to allow the attackers to shut down our online banking platform and allow it to be unavailable during our anticipated 14:00 to 17:00 outage.

To add additional scrutiny and anxiety for the executives, these plans had to be presented to the US Treasury and our financial regulators, which gave the executive team concern that we would be placed under supervisory letters if our decisions were steadfast. The cyber intelligence analysis from months of attack data was also provided to the Treasury and Regulators so they too could understand that the attackers usually turned off their attacks at 17:00 and that our exposure and loss rate was consistent with our risk models. It was the first time the organization's executives and management felt like they were making cybersecurity decisions and this grew my cyber intelligence program by leaps and bounds. Our intelligence estimates were off by thirty minutes, and we were back online transacting by 17:15 the same day. As the attacks were not subsiding through the spring of that year, the executive team, armed with the information from the collaborative efforts of the fusion team and the cyber intelligence analysis, made the decision to purchase the technology and reduce the financial losses even further. That organization is still using that same approach to mitigating other risks and how they purchase technology today as part of their risk management strategy. By leveraging this proven CI-DR framework it will enhance your cyber program from a pure technology thought to an operational risk program.

Figure I.1 shows how the CI-DR framework is designed and organized to address and provide reporting to directors and executives, to the risk

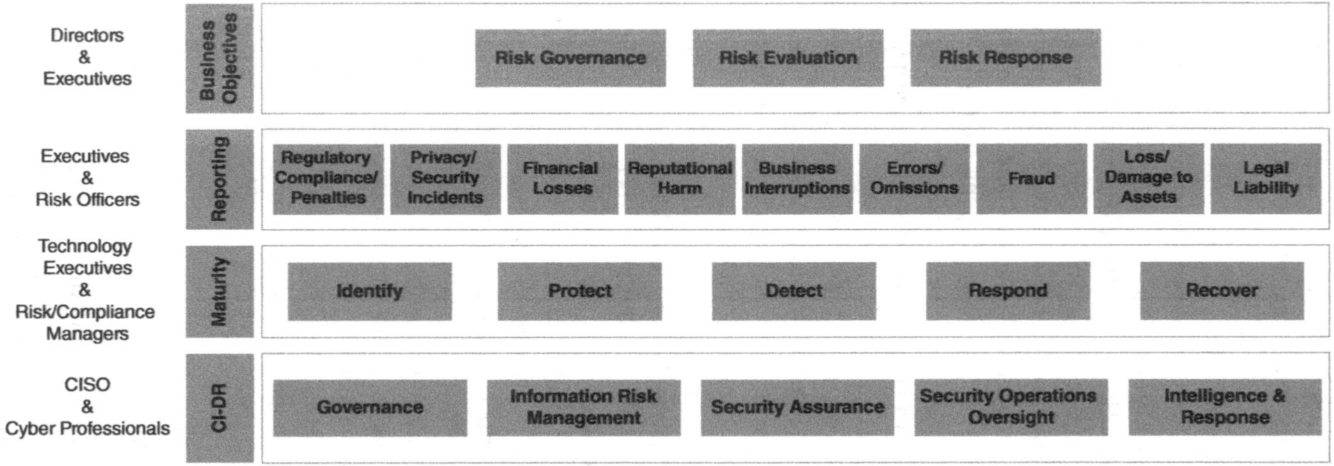

FIGURE I.1 CI-DR's business value.

Business Objectives	Risk Governance		Risk Evaluation	Risk Response		
Reporting	Regulatory Compliance/ Penalties	Privacy/ Security Incidents	Financial Losses	Reputational Harm	Business Interruptions	Errors/ Omissions	Fraud	Loss/ Damage to Assets	Legal Liability
Maturity	Identify		Protect	Detect	Respond		Recover
CI-DR	Governance		Information Risk Management	Security Assurance	Security Operations Oversight		Intelligence & Response

Directors & Executives

Executives & Risk Officers

Technology Executives & Risk/Compliance Managers

CISO & Cyber Professionals

officers and auditors, and of course to the leadership of the technology and cybersecurity functions within the company. The reporting to the directors and executives mostly covers the areas of what the cyber program is doing to enhance or contribute to how the organization governs and responds to risk. In many organizations the business objectives drive how the organization handles risk and are key to how the CI-DR framework ties its goals and missions to assisting the business in meeting those objectives. Committees are another area where the CI-DR program provides analysis and input for reporting. As we mentioned, consequences of loss are listed in the International Standards Organization's Risk Management standard and that taxonomy can be used to provide a one-to-many or many-to-many from CI-DR capabilities and functions to a risk mitigation process, technology, or exposure. Risk management and compliance professionals are businesspeople, and they need to have technologists speak a common language to help them also protect the organization against risk. The CI-DR also provides for compliance, internal auditors, and technology leadership with the ability to report on the maturity and performance of the functions and capabilities. Maturity reporting within the CI-DR framework gives the various organizations using this framework the confidence to not have to compare themselves to others, to determine their needs based on size and budget and skills available in the area, as well as providing the overall understanding that cybersecurity is an operational risk that can be understood by non-technologists.

We are positive that after reading this body of work the reader could confidently address the committees, the boards, and the executives when they ask about how the organization is governing its cyber risks. We know this framework has been able to address questions from regulators about the processes and the strategy for identifying, containing, and mitigating emergent cyber threats. Finally, if you are a director and an officer of a company implementing a CI-DR, the framework provides the formalization necessary to show that the organization's risk response and process and the directors and officers have done their due care to protect the company.

NOTES

- During a cyber incident is not the time to prepare your actions. Preparations are necessary; just as you prepare for financial loss, cyber incidents impact both operations and financial losses.

- Cybersecurity decisions with CI-DR "knowledge" become sophisticated business decisions.
- When cybersecurity leaders speak of business risks coupled with cyber intelligence analysis, any leader can make informed decisions.
- Any cyberattack can be thought of using deprived values and costs, which makes it an operational risk, which is ultimately a business risk. In this case, it was potential market risks, credit risks, and liquidity risks that could be lost due to operational loss. The organization wanted to keep our AA rating, and it didn't want to have customers leave to go to other institutions for banking, and it certainly did not want to take a substantial financial loss from either revenue, fines, or litigation.

A CI-DR program can have massive impacts and outcomes, as it is built with the purpose of delivering decisions to business leaders. Throughout this book, you will see the terms "information security" or "cybersecurity" used, and in CI-DR there are distinct differences, but for the purposes of this book these terms will be synonymous.

Cyber Intelligence-Driven Risk

CHAPTER ONE

Objectives of a Cyber Intelligence-Driven Risk Program

Knowledge must become capability.

– Carl von Clausewitz, Prussian general

A NY FRAMEWORK, methodology, or process has to have objectives and outcomes. The CI-DR™ program strives to achieve two objectives. First, the program provides accurate, timely, and relevant knowledge about cyber adversaries and the digital environment in which it operates. Adversaries within the cyber ecosystem are internal or external. An internal cyber adversary could be an employee, contractor, or someone with an objective and the physical or logical access to information otherwise not known to the public. External cyber adversaries include malicious actors, nation-states, competitors, or even outsourced platforms or processing environments and those employed or influenced there.

To achieve the first objective of the CI-DR program, there are four tasks that are required to be performed. First, the program must evaluate the existing cyber conditions, cyber risks, and potential operational losses from cyber events and incidents while taking into account the many internal or external adversarial capabilities holistically. Second, based on existing cyber conditions and cyber capabilities, the program estimates possible cyber adversarial courses of action and provides insight into possible future actions. Third, the program aids in identifying vulnerabilities that could be exploited by adversaries and the operational impact it can have on the organization. Fourth, the program and the "knowledge" created assists in the development and evaluation of the organization's courses of action for decisions based on the first three tasks.

The second objective of the CI-DR program is to protect organizations, through cyber counterintelligence activities, intending to deny adversaries valuable information about an organization's situation. These two objectives demonstrate how the CI-DR cyber risk programs support both the exploitative and protective elements necessary to operate in today's digital economy and infrastructure. The program aims to create timely and meaningful images of the situation confronting the decision-maker. CI-DR is the analysis and synthesis of information into knowledge. CI-DR cyber intelligence is "knowledge" that is distinguished from information or data, in that few pieces of information speak for themselves conclusively but must be combined and compared with other pieces of information, analyzed, evaluated, and given meaning.[1] Good cyber intelligence does not simply repeat the information that a source may reveal. Rather, it develops this raw material in order to tell us what that information means and identifies the implications for decision-making.[2]

The two objectives of the CI-DR program are created with simplicity that establishes the boundaries for how the program will operate and the areas in which it will collect information to provide value back to the organization's decision-makers. Additionally, the objectives provide executives and directors with a high-level understanding about what the program goals are, how they can be leveraged, and how they are connected with business leadership, and ultimately what analysis can be expected to support business objectives. The four tasks associated with the first objective provides the initial measurement of whether the options available are feasible or risky. To be able to describe a complete intelligence picture that provides us everything we need to know about a given situation, we would need that description to include knowledge of established conditions that have existed in the past, unfolding conditions as they exist in the present, and conditions which may exist in the future. Our complete image of what has been, what is, and what might be provides us with two classes of intelligence. The first is descriptive cyber intelligence, which describes existing and previously existing conditions. The second class, which attempts to anticipate future possibilities and probabilities, is estimative cyber intelligence.[3]

---

[1] US Government, Marine Corps Doctrinal Publication 2-Intelligence, (GAO) 1997.
[2] Ibid.
[3] US Government, Marine Corps Doctrinal Publication 2-Intelligence, (GAO) 1997.

This initial measurement does not have to be exact or futuristic, and doesn't have to be either qualitative or quantitative. What it does have to be is factual, and without bias or opinion, specifically when leadership is expecting intelligence and options on a particular subject.

Our CI-DR example for this chapter shows how the frame can support a business decision. Suppose a business leader wants to move an application from the organization's on-premises location to having it hosted at an outsourced provider (i.e. software as a service, platform as a service, or infrastructure as a service). The CI-DR program would begin with the analysis and collection of risk information from the current cyber environment as the baseline. A question would be posed to the team by the business leader, such as: "Is it safer to move existing system from on-premises to an externally hosted provider?" Additionally, the CI-DR program would collect and ingest into the CI-DR's cyber intelligence life cycle–specific information, cyber risks, vulnerabilities, cyber threats, costs, regulatory issues, and other relevant information to analyze and evaluate the various options where the leader wants to move the application. The result for this example could provide two or three options for providers and their risk ratings from a cyber intelligence perspective; they would also incorporate those ratings with the financial review of the provider, giving the business decision-maker the impact, risks, and profit or loss financial information for their review. The business leader is now able make better informed decisions about the outcome of their course of action, and to articulate and defend their position to senior leadership or the board of directors. The CI-DR program is not a stand-alone program. Discussed in the upcoming chapters, the program must have the right capabilities and resources available to evaluate the information collected and analyzed, with the ability to provide risks, options, and decision structures that can be generated for any consumer or leader within the organization. The decisions could be as simple as a "go or no-go" comparison chart or as complicated as total costs of ownership, potential losses, potential savings, or increased revenues, all with cyber risks included.

The second objective is not overly difficult to implement, but many U.S. commercial businesses are not as familiar with this approach as would military commanders be and maybe a few foreign countries that leverage cyber counterintelligence methods regularly. We can recall from our denial-of-service attack example against the banks in the Introduction that some organizations did leverage cyber counterintelligence and cyber deception methods to move the attacker's mindset into thinking they crippled the bank, thereby having them focus and move on to other targets while the banks resumed operations and returned to online activities that same day. Additionally, while U.S. businesses do protect their information from cyber adversaries in more traditional approaches, the cyber counterintelligence objective is a new concept for many businesses, except for a few of the Fortune 100 organizations.

Within the CI-DR functions and capabilities the cyber counterintelligence capability can be used within commercial businesses for mergers and acquisitions, for protecting information systems security strategies, or as part of the overall use of deception technologies or information to gain advantages in proactively identifying what cyber adversaries might be searching for within your networks. Organizations can test their cyber deceptive capabilities through tasks such as "red-teaming" activities. Red-teaming is usually performed by external organizations with the overall objective of gaining access to your facilities, systems, and data, and reporting on physical and digital compromises. The deceptive technologies are useful in validating those activities, as they could lead the testing team to encounter the deception systems and give them false information. Implementing the cyber counterintelligence portion of the CI-DR program will assist organizations in determining reconnaissance activities from adversaries, and assist with appropriate business or technology strategies to counter known cyber adversarial techniques, technologies, and processes. Organizations are performing some type of counterintelligence activity all the time, through marketing, delaying of products based on market research, keeping startups in "stealth," or by controlling access and release of information about their strategy or business processes. The counterintelligence activities are there, but the term or rational connection to that term has not been formally used for cyber activities. We are asking the reader to accept that the CI-DR cyber counterintelligence–type practices are occurring in organizations and to accept our usage of the term as not just a military action or function.

For example, passive cyber counterintelligence measures are designed to conceal, deceive, and deny information to adversaries, whether internal or external. Many businesses today do this by creating shared folders or locations where access is restricted to certain individuals. These folders are created by thinking about the content, the sensitivity, or the regulatory requirements to keep them separate to a select few. However, many businesses have missed the key components of restricting that information by not implementing either concealment or deceptive tactics to protect, restrict, and identify who may be trying to access the information, thereby usually providing a false sense of protection.

Another key objective for formally recognizing and having cyber counterintelligence as part of the CI-DR program is to protect personnel from subversion and acts of hostilities. Again, many organizations have travel security programs for executives and key personnel, implement phishing training and education, have evacuation drills, and provide some type of education for active shooters, etc., but again do not formally embrace the counterintelligence benefit or create formal counterintelligence objectives. An easy formal objective of using counterintelligence could be to protect facilities (i.e. removing signs for data centers or key processing facilities, etc.) and material against sabotage (internal, external, or even competitors). The full measures of counterintelligence can include security of restricted material, personnel security, physical security, security education, communications security, data security, electromagnetic emission security (i.e. Bluetooth, Wi-Fi, NFC, Bonjour, etc.), and censorship.[4] The overlooked counterintelligence objective can be useful and provide value to industries such as financial services, manufacturing, utilities, pharmaceuticals, insurance, social media, and many others that are often overlooked as critical infrastructure or social services.

Another key concept we want the reader to understand is that a CI-DR program should not be thought of just as a product, but also as the processes which produce specific needed knowledge in order to make better business decisions. Process activities and capabilities are driven by the need to answer questions that are crucial to both the tactical and strategic interests of the organization or to meet business objectives. A CI-DR program operates in an environment characterized by uncertainty and with it risks that must be understood and reduced by the decision-makers.

 NOTES

1. Cyber counterintelligence is a key objective for organizations to have and is built into the CI-DR framework.
2. Using this book can help with building guidelines to help you create a CI-DR program tailored to your organization and help build its charter and boundaries.
3. It is important to identify the formal boundaries for a CI-DR program due to all the interconnective functions and collection methods that a CI-DR program can touch.

[4] Marine Corps Combat Development Command, Doctrine Division, MCWP 2-14 Counterintelligence, 2 May 2016, https://www.marines.mil/Portals/59/Publications/MCWP%202-6%20W%20Erratum%20Counterintelligence.pdf

4. Organizations and individuals should consider cyber counterintelligence and cyber deception programs if they already have a mature cybersecurity strategy aligned with business objectives.
5. Cyber counterintelligence programs can be tasked with identifying faint digital signals being used in your organization to view information that has been deemed sensitive.
6. A CI-DR program with all of its functions and capabilities can help business leaders gain better decision-making knowledge about running a business today.

2

Importance of Cyber Intelligence for Businesses

Our knowledge of circumstances has increased, but our uncertainty, instead of having diminished, has only increased. The reason of this is that we do not gain all our experience at once, but by degrees; so our determinations continue to be assailed incessantly by fresh experience; and the mind, if we may use the expression, must always be under arms.

– Carl von Clausewitz, Prussian general

W E READ PREVIOUSLY that the CI-DR™ program has two objectives and a few tasks that create the interactions and the "connective tissue" between both command (leadership) and operations; its primary objective is to support decision-making by reducing uncertainty.[1] The traditional intelligence axiom of "knowledge is power" is the goal of the CI-DR

---

[1] US Government, Marine Corps Doctrinal Publication 2-Intelligence, (GAO) 1997.

program and that knowledge needs to support critical business decisions, specifically in our digital and cyber working environment. As a regularly attending contributor to a few boards of directors and as an advisor to other boards, the one area of concern I continue to identify is that many cybersecurity or IT security programs lack the business risk information with proper analysis when presenting to boards. This analysis and reporting of cyber risk requires the information provided to be articulated for discussion, be clearly understood by business executives, and be able to be debated in business terms with reinforceable facts to support the decisions made. How many readers of this book have been presented with technology vulnerabilities, only to see numbers and not understand the real intent or criticality of the information being presented? A CI-DR program provides businesses with the relevant information needed to make decisions. Do not think of providing vulnerabilities metrics as a negative report, but understand that it needs to be transformed into a report that is informing the business leader that a decision has to be made. That decision can be that we need to update our systems, the technology teams need time to reboot or restore a critical system, or that we will lose revenue due to particular identified compromises in that system. Reporting from cyber metrics to business has to be made clearer to those making decisions, and to those readers who are reporting vulnerabilities. Our CI-DR program cyber intelligence life cycle can be used to support how the functions and capabilities drive decision-making processes. The dissemination portion that produces the reporting or options is done without obfuscation of why those vulnerabilities being reported are important for the business leader to make decisions whether to ignore or action the report. (See Figure 2.1.)

The CI-DR program objectives provide an organization with guidance to assist in building a formal charter for the program, which can build rational processes of how the cyber data enters the life cycle and how analysis processes transform raw data to become "knowledge" and produce appropriate reporting in business terms. There is a ton of reporting being done today around cyber but most of it is done reactively and at the tactical level, meaning no business decisions are being made, and the information being reported is only valuable for use by a chief information security officer (CISO) or chief information officer (CIO) and is only used to make technology risk decisions. While this type of information is still valuable to the technician, as a risk or business leader you can most likely only use these tactical-level metrics and reporting as a way to find key performance indicators. The data or information at this stage in the cyber intelligence life cycle is still raw and provides no indicators of risk or useful information to business leaders.

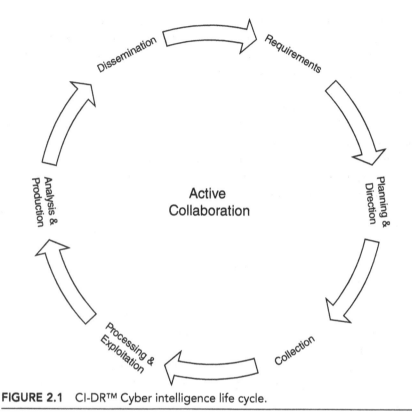

FIGURE 2.1 CI-DR™ Cyber intelligence life cycle.

We talk a lot about leveraging tradition intelligence concepts and processes within this book and our CI-DR cyber intelligence life cycle is a direct offspring of one of those concepts. Similar to traditional descriptions of the types of intelligence, the CI-DR types of cyber intelligence do not require much change to the definition or require advanced degrees in cybersecurity; it is, in fact, simplistic in nature. The two primary classes of the CI-DR cyber intelligence are "descriptive cyber intelligence" and "estimative cyber intelligence." Descriptive cyber intelligence has two components. "Basic cyber intelligence," which is the general background knowledge about established and relatively constant cyber conditions, is often encyclopedic in nature and often mundane. This information is easiest to gather, and is often available through open sources.[2] Basic cyber intelligence is usually not decisive in nature, like providing vulnerability metrics without analysis and trends. Descriptive cyber intelligence

---

[2] US Government, Marine Corps Doctrinal Publication 2-Intelligence, (GAO) 1997.

also includes "current cyber intelligence," which is concerned with describing the existing cyber situation. The differentiator between basic and current cyber intelligence is that current cyber intelligence describes more changeable factors. For example, if the organization has identified vulnerabilities within a certain system, but nothing yet has occurred to impact or exploit that system, this is basic cyber intelligence. However, if there is an exploit that leads to a compromise of the system from that identified vulnerability, this would be considered current cyber intelligence as the existing situation changed, and the intelligence is more time-sensitive for making a decision.

The second class of the CI-DR cyber intelligence is known as "estimative cyber intelligence," and is focused on potential developments. Estimative cyber intelligence is the most demanding and is the most important task of creating "knowledge" from raw digital intelligence, as it seeks to anticipate a possible future or several futures.[3] Just as military commanders cannot reasonably expect traditional estimative intelligence to precisely predict the future, estimative cyber intelligence deals with the realm of possibilities and probabilities. It is inherently the less reliable of the classes of intelligence because it is not based on what actually is or has been, but rather on what might occur.[4] A good example of estimative cyber intelligence is described in our real-world example in the Introduction.

As we continue to describe the types of cyber intelligence used in our CI-DR framework and program, it is important for the reader to understand that efforts to provide "knowledge" and decisions are complicated by the ability to assess cyber capabilities and estimate adversarial intentions, which can become a complication during the interpretation of the information collected. To develop objective and accurate cyber intelligence, we must understand this problem. We can examine it through a discussion of signals or indicators and noise.[5] Indicators or signals refer to information that can lead to valuable insight, whereas noise is simply useless information that interferes with identifying the truth. A good example of weeding through the noise can be found in the same example in our Introduction, where the QCF (Qassam Cyber Fighters) had been posting comments about their upcoming or past cyberattacks. This information was mostly false and extremely distracting, and misled or tainted much of the real intentions of their cyberattacks. Fortunately, there were clear signals and indicators that were being provided to see clearly through their many online rantings. However, the difference between true and

---

[3] US Government, Marine Corps Doctrinal Publication 2-Intelligence, (GAO) 1997.
[4] Ibid.
[5] Ibid.

false information is rarely easy to distinguish and the reader must take care to understand that effort must be made to differentiate.

As we continue to discuss the types of cyber intelligence and why the CI-DR uses these, we must also discuss the levels of intelligence. There are only three, to continue with simplicity, and these lead to our building cyber intelligence requirements in the upcoming chapters. The three levels of our CI-DR cyber intelligence types are strategic, operational, and tactical, in that order. Tactical cyber intelligence is the most fundamental, concerning location (i.e. geographical, networks, or internet protocols), capabilities (i.e. sophistication levels, skills, or method of delivery), and potential adversarial intent. Tactical cyber intelligence is the tactics, techniques, and procedures, or TTPs[6] used in the cyber threat intelligence capability of the CI-DR program. In cyber it is wise to take care and understand that this is where most of the attention of cyber defense is focused today. While the tactical level deserves attention, the problem with a singular focus at this level means that the adversary is either already in the network, or at the door of your gateway trying to get in. Yet, if appropriate resources were expended in the previous two levels, some of this tactical activity may be precluded and have better usage by business leaders for decisions.[7] The Security Operations Center (SOC) is fundamentally where tactical activities occur and will be discussed in a later chapter.

Operational cyber intelligence is the level at which campaigns and major operations are planned, conducted, and sustained.[8] At the operational level, malicious actors plan their campaigns based upon what they have learned in collecting their own cyber intelligence and on what they had surmised as being necessary based upon their strategic goals. Actors build the capabilities (botnets, malware, delivery methodology [phishing], etc.) needed to support the tactical operations. They maneuver in cyberspace (hop points) to position capability where they need to in order to be effective in their tactical missions. This is the level where a hacktivist group may plan both cyber and physical world activities to support their objectives.[9] Examples of operational-level cyber intelligence could be the following:

- Trend analysis indicating the technical direction in which an adversary's capabilities are evolving.

---

[6] US Government, Marine Corps Warfighting Publication 2-14 Counterintelligence, GAO, 2002.
[7] Elizabeth Finan, INSA, Operational Levels of Cyber Intelligence, "Cyber Intelligence Taskforce," 2013.
[8] US Government, Joint Publication 1-02, "Department of Defense Dictionary of Military and Associated Terms," 2016, http://www.dtic.mil/doctrine/dod_dictionary.
[9] Elizabeth Finan, INSA, Operational Levels of Cyber Intelligence, "Cyber Intelligence Taskforce," 2013.

- Indications that an adversary has selected an avenue of approach for targeting your organization.
- Indications that an adversary is building capability to exploit a particular avenue of approach.
- The revelation of adversary tactics, techniques, and procedures.
- Understanding of the adversary operational cycle (i.e. decision-making, acquisitions, command-and-control [C2] methods for both the technology and the personnel).
- Technical, social, legal, financial, or other vulnerabilities that the adversary has.
- Information that enables the defender to influence an adversary as they move through the process of executing their intent and actions (i.e. attack chain).[10]

The strategic level of cyber activity is the determination of objectives and guidance by the highest organizational entity representing a group or organization and their use of the group or organization's resources toward achievement of those objectives. This is the level where the business executive officers and directors provide direction, guidance, and requests or requirements for knowledge based on business objectives. Examples of strategic cyber intelligence might include:

- The decision by a competitor or potential competitor to enter your market space (e.g. a foreign competitor's new five-year plan now shows interest in developing a domestic capability in a technology your company is known for).
- Indications that a competitor, or foreign government, may have previously acquired intellectual property via cyber exploitation.
- Indications that a competitor, or foreign government, is establishing an atypical influential relationship with a portion of your supply chain.
- Indications that your corporate strategic objectives may be threatened due to adversarial cyber activity.[11]

Now that we have structured the type, levels, and some examples of cyber intelligence we have to take that information and make it knowledge, which

---

[10] Ibid.
[11] Elizabeth Finan, INSA, Operational Levels of Cyber Intelligence, "Cyber Intelligence Taskforce," 2013.

means analysis. There are many books, university courses, whitepapers, and frameworks that detail many of the various analysis tools and techniques. I am only going to list a few and will not go into the detail of what method is better than another; the reader should be aware of the various types to prepare them for the types of reports they may receive. Below is a list that the United Kingdom's National Intelligence Model uses and provides a good framework for a detailed list of products and purposes for different types of analysis.[12]

- Results Analysis – this process provides gaps, best practices, or may be used as an After-Action Report (AAR).
- Pattern Analysis – can be used to provide management decisions for tactical or operational prioritization, or may be used to identify emerging threats, trends, and new requirements.
- Market Analysis – can be used to see if there is proliferation of tools, techniques, processes (TTPs) for sale, and may be used by management to provide prioritization of remediation activities, or operational enhancements in defending their organization.
- Demographics and Social Trend Analysis – can be used by management to highlight future pressures, used for incident planning and response activities based on emerging social phenomena or sensitivities.
- Malicious/Criminal Business Profiles – can be used by management for understanding key points of operational disruption, the need for new regulations or legislation, change in resources to meet the threat, or to ensure the organization has training to meet new threats (i.e. phishing, malware, social engineering, etc.)
- Network Analysis – can be used by management strategically as an indicator for the seriousness of an activity. Can also be used tactically and operationally to understand operational losses, highlights gaps, and provide potential targets within the organization.
- Risk Analysis – can be used by management to create risk management planning (i.e. impact, probability, consequences both financially and reputational, etc.). Provides the prelude to prioritizing actions, at both the strategic and operational levels.
- Target Profile Analysis – TTPs of the malicious actor or group, informs which targets will most likely be attacked, and provides decisions about how resources can be deployed to mitigate the attack.

---

[12] United Nations Office of Drugs and Crime, Criminal Intelligence Manual for Analysts, United Nations, NY, 2011.

- Operational Intelligence Analysis – can be used by management to prevent mission creep or scope creep, prioritization of intelligence work, needs, or requirements stemming from current intelligence.

The use of the CI-DR cyber intelligence life cycle, the types of analysis, and the dissemination of knowledge to business leadership is how our program works in conjunction with the overall approach of having functions and capabilities and can inform, guide, direct, and provide the ability to adapt and prioritize for any change or emerging threat to an organization.

NOTES

- The CISOs and CIOs are not necessarily involved with strategic directions for the organization, but need to be informed so that cyber intelligence "knowledge" can be created to support the strategy.
- Business leaders when creating critical or priority cyber intelligence requirements (CIRs or PIRs) should be aware of the type of analysis and usage that can contribute to decisions.
- The CI-DR cyber intelligence process is a proven method taken from the military intelligence process that provides a repeatable method of reporting but may require further iterations or new processes for different organizations.
- Business leaders should be disciplined in not getting too much involved in the tactical level of cyber intelligence but should focus on prioritization and direction at the operational and strategic levels of cyber intelligence.

CHAPTER THREE

Military to Commercial Viability of the CI-DR™ Program

The government spends millions on designing tools, capabilities, and intelligence platforms to support the defense of a nation. The same concepts and functions can be leveraged without the cost to defend a commercial entity, as many are casualties of nation-state targeting.

– Cyber Commander's Handbook[1]

L ET'S PREPARE your thinking with another real-world event. This is taken from the activities of the Electronic Disturbance Theater to emphasize how malicious organizations can be disruptive and what began as the National Strategy to Secure Cyberspace.

A small group of activists, known as the Electronic Disturbance Theater (EDT), supported the Zapatista movement. A typical scenario for the EDT was to

---

[1] Kevin Colman, *Cyber Commanders Handbook*, Association for Computing Machinery, 2013 v 4.

publicize an attack weeks before the actual event. They used chat rooms, Internet advertisements, and computer conferences to promote their next Floodnet attack and gain publicity. To increase its effectiveness, the EDT signed up thousands of participants for their Floodnet attacks. In April 1998, the Floodnet program attacked Mexican President Zedillo's website, quickly crashing the server. More attacks continued during the summer of 1998, to include the Mexican Interior Ministry and Mexican Embassy in England with the largest event planned for September 9, 1998. Bulletins were released in late August and EDT publicized the impending attack with their Open-Ex exhibit at the Art Festival in Linz, Austria, during this time. The intended targets were President Zedillo, the Frankfurt Stock Exchange, and the Defense Information Systems Agency (DISA).

Since these were publicized "performances," DISA was concerned as to how to thwart these attacks. There were many inquiries by United States military personnel into Floodnet and the EDT during this period in order to gain knowledge about the purpose of the attack and the nature of the Floodnet applet itself. When the actual attack occurred on September 9, DISA was ready to defend its network. A system administrator at DISA changed the Perl script on the Floodnet applet, which in effect became an electronic countermeasure effort and in some eyes, an offensive act. This new applet shut down the web browsers of the users who were supporting the attack by EDT.[2]

Military intelligence (MI) has been a part of war fighting since the dawn of humanity. This book does not cover the entire history of how MI evolved, but instead quickly jumps into the era of using cyber intelligence as it became necessary to meet new threats in the digital ecosystems of both government and commercial organizations. The National Strategy to Secure Cyberspace identifies eight major actions and initiatives for cyberspace security response:

1. Establish a public–private architecture for responding to national-level cyber incidents.
2. Provide for the development of tactical and strategic analysis of cyberattacks and vulnerability assessments.
3. Encourage the development of a private sector capability to share a synoptic view of the health of cyberspace.
4. Expand the Cyber Warning and Information Network to support the role of DHS in coordinating crisis management for cyberspace security.
5. Improve national incident management.

---

[2] Ibid.

6. Coordinate processes for voluntary participation in the development of national public–private continuity and contingency plans.
7. Exercise cybersecurity continuity plans for federal systems.
8. Improve and enhance public–private information sharing involving cyber-attacks, threats, and vulnerabilities.[3]

In addition to the National Strategy to Secure Cyberspace, both the U.S. Army and the U.S. Airforce have adapted their doctrine publications to emphasize the need for leveraging knowledge beyond the classical military intelligence models. The U.S. Army ARDP 2-0 states that the intelligence warfighting function is larger than military intelligence. Critical participants within the warfighting function include commanders, decision-makers, all staff members, and intelligence leaders. The use of the intelligence leader is new to the doctrine. It refers to a larger group of military intelligence professionals than just senior leaders and commanders. Intelligence leaders are intended to address all military intelligence professionals who lead and supervise intelligence soldiers, regardless of age, rank, or echelon. Additionally, the U.S. Airforce AFDD 3-12 identifies that the proliferation of commercially available technology will allow adversaries to develop niche capabilities that will threaten, in varying degrees, the successful conduct of operations in areas where U.S. forces were previously unchallenged. Space and cyber networks are increasingly vulnerable to a wide array of new threats. Adversary anti-access capabilities will continue to improve, challenging U.S. ability to project power and influence. Countering these capabilities is vital to assure freedom of action in, through, and from air, space, and cyberspace.

As we read in earlier chapters the goal of the CI-DR™ program is to provide decisions to leaders, but this cannot be done in isolation or pushing concerns upward without understanding what the business leader or leadership needs or wants to know. In the military and government sectors this is called the Commander's Critical Information Requirements (CCIRs). As we learned previously about the levels of intelligence, the strategic and operational levels are where the organization's directors and business executives create requests for knowledge based on objectives and strategic planning. CCIRs are a list of information required by the commander critical to facilitating timely decision-making that affects successful mission accomplishment. It has a few key subcomponents which will be explained in business terms as well. These key subcomponents are:

---

[3] U.S. Government, *National Strategy to Secure Cyberspace*, White House, 2003.

- Critical Friendly Force Information. Friendly information with an anticipated and stated priority for planning and decision-making. This information can be about strategic partnerships, supply chain vendors, or processes and processing done by others.
- Priority Intelligence Requirements (PIR). Intel requirements with an anticipated and stated priority for planning and decision-making. This information can be about new technologies, threats, business options, impacts to operations, etc.

Historically, CCIRs have focused upon intelligence requirements identified by the CCTF (Commander, Combined Task Force) and thus the C2 (Command-and-Control section) was the primary staff for development of CCIRs. Within a "systems planning approach" to a crisis, CCIRs expand to cover intelligence and information requirements for decision-making. This requires the additional direct support of the C5 (policy), C7 (civil-military), and POLAD (political advisor) to fully outline the CCIR.[4] Figure 3.1 takes the lessons and concepts from traditional intelligence capabilities and uses them in our CI-DR function to produce cyber CIRs and cyber PIRs.

As mentioned, in a commercial organization, the term "friendly force information" could be information from vendors, partners, industry associations, or joint resilience and assistance programs that were defined to assist organizations in supporting continuous operations. For example, the financial services industry processing organizations utilize and test resilient processing support in the event that one processor can no longer operate. These processors test their resiliency through programs like Quantum Dawn,[5] and others. In the health-care industry, we see this with associations of doctors supporting different hospitals based on their skills, supporting overflow for bed counts, and other joint operational support components. The lessons learned from military operations are being used in many industries but may not be well known to business leaders or have been implemented in other industries, which places many organizations at risk for continued operations. You will read in the following chapters why there is a need, as a business leader, to embrace CCIRs and PIRs. Your head of risk or information security should be asking for your guidance and requirements; if they have not asked, seek them out and provide a list of requirements that you would want to know in the event of a cyber incident.

---

[4] Kevin Colman, *Cyber Commanders Handbook*, Association for Computing Machinery, 2013 v 4.
[5] Security Industries and Financial Markets Association, Cybersecurity Exercise: Quantum Dawn, 2018, https://www.sifma.org/resources/general/cybersecurity-exercise-quantum-dawn-iv/.

	Function
Critical Intelligence Requirements	
CIR 1	Cyber threats to the organization's infrastructure. Coordination and Intelligence requires all information that helps identify foreign and domestic entities or organizations responsible for directing, planning, or conducting computer network operations against the organization's computer or telecommunications network and systems.
Priority Intelligence Requirements	
PIR 1	Evidence of malicious actors, groups, nation-states, single entities, or other anti-U.S. terrorist groups or associations (including adversarial state agents or criminals) acting as a focal point for computer network attack development.
IR1.1	Names, locations, key personnel, and structure of malicious organization.
PIR 1.2	Intentions, plans, and capabilities to conduct computer or systems attack against organization, organization's facilities, or infrastructure.
IR1.2.1	Administrative and operational relationships, including roles and functions, decision-making processes, operational procedures, and contingency planning.
IR1.2.2	Prevalence of Computer Network Attack (CNA) or Computer Network Exploitation (CNE) (e.g. scans, probes, downloads, and IP mapping efforts) into sector networks or systems by country, geo-location, domain name, IP address, or BGP neighbors.
IR1.2.3	Quantity and nature of downloaded information by country, domain, IP, etc.
IR1.2.4	Quantity and nature of any phishing or social engineering activity targeting this sector.
IR1.2.5	Evidence of specifically placed malware, loggers, etc. that results in data lost, compromised, or controlled.
PIR 1.3	Unusual or unauthorized attempts to download or obtain offensive toolkits that have yet to be identified as malicious.
PIR 1.4	Foreign or domestic commercial, government-owned, or known front companies that support external malicious organizations in acquiring CNA/CNE technologies.
PIR 1. 5	Foreign or domestic universities, institutes, research facilities, or development facilities associated or affiliated with known malicious organizations or members.
PIR 1.6	Malware production facilities, or other computer technology related organizations affiliated with known malicious organizations or members.
PIR 1.6.1	Identity of known or suspected malware authors and country of origin.
PIR 1.7	Malicious groups, individuals, websites, or chat rooms that have openly expressed support to other malicious groups, organizations, or members.

FIGURE 3.1 Critical intelligence requirements.

Without proper planning, requesting key requirements for knowledge, and formal guidance from leadership, organizations are working and making decisions with limited facts, or are being provided information that is useless. CI-DR can facilitate ensuring data is factual, useful, and timely for a leader's consumption into their decision-making process. History continues to be repeated in cyberspace, as there is a lack of education in business courses around cyber risks and a major disconnect between executive leadership and cybersecurity professionals due to jargon and technical information provided with no business context. For a historical progression from military to commercial cyberattacks, and to provide business readers with some knowledge of why their organizations are at risk, we begin with some examples of how cyberattacks against commercial organizations in the late 1990s and early 2000s were primarily disruptive, or malicious code was implanted to commit fraud. The government and its supply chain on the other hand were attacked primarily using advanced techniques for operational disruption and information stealing to gain first-strike capabilities in the event of war. Below are some very interesting publicized attacks where the reader can easily identify the aggression, escalation, and increased sophistication over the years that has turned from military to commercial. These examples provide emphasis on outsourced, supply chain, and partnerships especially within digital and cyber defensive ecosystems.

The name Moonlight Maze[6] refers to an incident in which U.S. officials accidentally discovered a pattern of probing of computer systems at the Pentagon, NASA, United States Department of Energy, private universities, and research labs that had begun in March 1998 and had been going on for nearly two years. Sources report that the invaders were systematically marauding through tens of thousands of files, including maps of military installations, troop configurations, and military hardware designs. The United States Department of Defense traced the trail back to a mainframe computer in the former Soviet Union, but the sponsor of the attacks is unknown, and Russia denies any involvement. Moonlight Maze was still being actively investigated by U.S. intelligence agencies in 2003. The importance to the business reader is that the attack demonstrates the adversary's quest for information and their reconnaissance activities probing for additional weaknesses within computer systems. Not only did it hit direct military installations and systems, but the attack also spanned private institutions doing work on behalf of a military

---

[6] Committee on Governmental Affairs, Testimony of James Adams, 2000, https://fas.org/irp/congress/2000_hr/030200_adams.htm.

program. The supply chain was not out of scope and was instrumental in identifying backdoors or inappropriate access rights to other locations.

Another attack moved from direct military attacks to commercial contractors and vendors who produce goods and services to the military. Titan Rain was the designation given by the federal government of the United States to a series of coordinated attacks on American computer systems since 2003; they were known to have been ongoing for at least three years. The attacks were labeled as Chinese in origin, although their precise nature, e.g. state-sponsored espionage, corporate espionage, or random hacker attacks, and their real identities – masked by proxy, zombie computer, spyware/virus infected – remain unknown. The activity known as "Titan Rain" is believed to be associated with an advanced persistent threat. In early December 2005 the director of the SANS Institute, a security institute in the United States, said that the attacks were "most likely the result of Chinese military hackers attempting to gather information on U.S. systems." Titan Rain hackers gained access to many United States defense contractor computer networks that were targeted for their sensitive information, including those at Lockheed Martin, Sandia National Laboratories, Redstone Arsenal, and NASA. The business readers should understand that attacking military installations and systems was difficult and time intensive, but by the very nature of how the supply chains were built, the partnership sharing of information, and the access granted from one system to another, the attackers were able to maneuver and learn more about weaknesses and ways to bridge systems and networks.

Estonia was the first country to be hit by cyberattack from an adversarial nation that disagreed with some of its statements and actions. The cyberattack began on 27 April 2007, and swamped websites of Estonian organizations, including the Estonian Parliament, banks, ministries, newspapers and broadcasters, amid the country's row with Russia about the relocation of the Bronze Soldier of Tallinn, an elaborate Soviet-era grave marker, as well as war graves in Tallinn. Some observers reckoned that the onslaught on Estonia was of a sophistication not seen before. The case is studied intensively by many countries and military planners as, at the time it occurred, it may have been the second-largest instance of state-sponsored cyberwarfare, following Titan Rain. The business importance here is that many of our midsized corporations have annual revenues larger than Estonia's GDR and if a country that has a good military can be completely taken offline and halt operations, this is the silver bullet that businesses need to be concerned with. Coordinated cyberattacks to halt operations, not just disrupt, can place your business in a position of bankruptcy and potential closure or restructuring. I am not promoting fear, uncertainty, and doubt regarding this attack, but wish to raise the level of awareness that countries have been taken offline, and that focusing on ensuring resiliency for your company is a top priority.

GhostNet 2008 is the name given by researchers at the Information Warfare Monitor to a large-scale cyber spying operation discovered in March 2009. Its command-and-control infrastructure is based mainly in the People's Republic of China and has infiltrated high-value political, economic, and media locations in 103 countries. Computer systems belonging to embassies, foreign ministries, and other government offices, and the Dalai Lama's Tibetan exile centers in India, London, and New York City were compromised. This is a great example of how cyber can be leveraged for espionage activities; if you are a business that may have particular groups disenfranchised, or competition is steep in your industry, specifically crafted malicious code could be leveraged to spy on corporate activities. As a business reader, you should think about and request information about the safety of your mergers or acquisitions, who has access to your corporate strategy, and whether there are any external conversations about new marketing or product launches that would impact your business should that information find its way to the public. Note that we specifically cover the value of protecting mergers and acquisitions through the CI-DR program in a later chapter based on the author's past experiences.

Operation Aurora was a cyberattack conducted by advanced persistent threats by activists such as the Elderwood Group based in Beijing, China, with ties to the People's Liberation Army. First publicly disclosed by Google on January 12, 2010, in a blog post, the attack began in mid-2009 and continued through December 2009. The attack has been aimed at dozens of other organizations, of which Adobe Systems, Juniper Networks, and Rackspace have publicly confirmed that they were targeted. According to media reports, Yahoo, Symantec, Northrop Grumman, Morgan Stanley, and Dow Chemical were also among the targets. As a result of the attack, Google stated in its blog that it plans to operate a completely uncensored version of its search engine in China "within the law, if at all," and acknowledged that if this is not possible it may leave China and close its Chinese offices. Official Chinese media responded stating that the incident is part of a U.S. government conspiracy. This should be of interest to the business reader here from the outcome of this cyberattack. China now operates its own version of Google, has developed its own antivirus and malware applications, and now challenges Juniper and other network hardware products with its own Huawei hardware to compete in this market. These attacks have filled company voids in China, allowing them to provide similar services built by China for the Chinese population and sell to others for lower retail value; we define this activity as market disruption, saturation, and competition through illegal means.

Commercial business leaders can leverage much of what military commanders and government leaders have had at their disposal for centuries. However, many of the commercial business leaders have not had the formal education and training during their careers to leverage this valuable asset; this is why the CI-DR program is instrumental in supporting new ways that business leaders make decisions. As you have been reading, cyberattacks have increased in scope and voracity, and expanded to companies where the leadership in the past thought they had nothing of value, and business operations were severely impacted. Every industry has an Information Sharing and Analysis Center and the information provided as part of the membership is worth the investment and time for your organization to become involved. It can assist in providing advanced knowledge of cyberattacks in your industry, support the collaboration and testing of resiliency, provide sharing of cybersecurity activities and best practices, and provide the organization with the ability to face these challenges together and not feel abandoned or helpless should a cyber incident severely impact how you conduct business.

The impacts that state-sponsored organizations have on non-military, non-governmental organizations is just as important for business leaders to understand. These attack techniques are quickly distributed to organized criminal groups that use the tools, techniques, and procedures for monetary or market entry gains. Do not be lulled into a false sense of security that government or military attacks will not impact your commercial organization. Take, for example, where we have gone from the STUXNET code to Not Petya and other attacks that pose threats to Supervisory Control and Data Acquisition (SCADA), Industrial Control Systems (ICS), and the Internet of Things (IoT). IoT is everything commercial, including vehicles, smart homes, smart appliances, etc., which impacts the commercial business leader.

NOTES

- The CI-DR program is impactful and with some advanced insight, facts, and analysis, the private sector cyber intelligence analyst can influence decisions, implement new controls, and protect the organization before malicious activities occur.

- Cyber intelligence in the private sector is similar to many government and military operational objectives, with these exceptions. The attacks against commercial targets are primarily motivated by money and intellectual property theft. Negatively impacting the organization would be a focus on greed-based motivations that do not support the good of the industry or good of the employees. For example, most cyber intelligence programs share anonymous threat indicators with other members within an Information Sharing and Analysis Center (ISAC); however, a company may make a choice not to share critical cybersecurity information with a competitor, even if they knew an attack may impact their overall revenues and use it as a competitive advantage.
- The U.S. Courts have declared that cybersecurity is not a competitive advantage and information must be shared.

CHAPTER FOUR

CI-DR™ Security Program Components

The world has a way of undermining complex plans. This is particularly true in fast-moving environments. A fast-moving environment can evolve more quickly than a complex plan can be adapted to it. By the time you have adapted, the target has changed.

– Carl von Clausewitz, Prussian general

AS WE CONTINUE with our real-world examples, as the leader of an organization, and while cybersecurity may report to another function, or even be outsourced, many business leaders are making decisions based on either compliance requirements, diversifying or acquiring assets, or changing business direction based on information that mostly excludes cyber intelligence, cyber risk, and cybersecurity information. By not including the cyber intelligence knowledge, information being presented will have errors, omissions, and will be devoid of the "business killer" data, which will lead to unknown exposures and loss of revenue from poor-decision making.

There is currently no faster-moving environment than cybersecurity in which two objects, velocity and capability of attack, can quickly undermine complex planning, in which environment a micro-agent can have a macro impact from anywhere in the world. Building a sustainable cyber intelligence-driven risk (CI-DR™) program has to be part of a larger embryonic cybersecurity program. The embryonic cybersecurity components or functional capabilities of the CI-DR program are simple in design and planning, and can stand alone as independent capabilities, but when combined through "connective tissue" the program can be adaptable and evolve to meet a fast-moving environment such as cyber. A single capability or all capabilities can be transformed to meet new cyber intelligence requirements, but a function remains consistent with meeting the functions' overall objectives. This section is an overview of functional capabilities, how the "connective tissue" of each capability provides key intelligence data to assist in effective decision support structures.

As stated above, a CI-DR program cannot be created or run as an independent process or function and must have foundational or skeletal capabilities and functions to support and assist in gathering and collecting information, remediating findings, and disseminating the created "knowledge" or the intelligence package. These foundational capabilities that provide the embryonic matrix or connective tissue are part of a specifically structured information/cybersecurity program, as it is within this program the CI-DR program is a substrate that is designated as the protector of the organization. This approach to designing information/cybersecurity programs has been in the making over the past twenty years and has been implemented in many Fortune 500 companies in some shape or form. Your organization may not be in the Fortune 500 listings for size and revenue, but cybersecurity impacts every organization, and you can also leverage this CI-DR program to benefit your organization and take advantage of applying this approach to your company and cybersecurity programs. As you will read, many of these functions are consistent somewhere within most organizations, with naming conventions different but objectives similar. These functions and capabilities have been gathered, condensed, and implemented from a majority of the regulatory and industry best practices across the globe. You will see that from this skeletal structure, controls, processes, and capabilities found within these publications to name a few: FFIEC IT Handbooks, MAS 200, NYDFS, CSC, NIST NICE, NIST SP 800-53, and the NIST CSF. These functions and capabilities provide an organization the ability to review, audit, mature, and deploy the proper people, processes, and technologies to create a CI-DR program tailored to your organization. (See Figure 4.1.)

1. Stratum 0, the CORE capabilities, addresses what the organization has to have by asking, "What is of value to the company?" "How can those valuables be lost?" and "How do you protect those valuables?" It is a continual identification of the crown jewels and the applicable protections. Stratum 0 approach has identified approximately 150*** possible controls.
2. Stratum 1 builds on the core capabilities by establishing further foundational requirements for an even more refined identification of "What is of value to the company?" "How can those valuables be lost?" and "How do you protect those valuables?" Simply, it is the identification of crown jewels and the applicable protections. The Stratum 1 approach has identified approximately 97*** possible controls.
3. Stratum 2 rounds out the "must have" capabilities that an established-level mature cyber/information security program must have. The Stratum 2 approach has identified approximately 83*** possible controls.
4. Stratum 3 is where the enterprise as a whole is making decisions based on cyber/information security information. This would include changes to how technologies are evaluated and procured, and what risks may need additional capital reserves. The Stratum 3 approach has identified approximately 58*** possible controls.
5. Stratum 4 is where the enterprise is involved in identifying and making decisions based upon cyber/information security risks. Clearly established roles and responsibilities are defined through the three lines of defense, and clear segregation of duties between IT and cyber/information security has been formalized. New technologies are proactively pursued and deployed to meet business objectives while reducing cyber risks, and data is used to evaluate and select process improvements throughout the organization. The Stratum 4 approach has identified approximately 43*** possible controls.

    ***Controls can vary depending on the organization's cyber risk appetite.

To build a CI-DR program we need to define the basic functions that an information or cybersecurity program should have at a minimum for building, reporting, evaluating, and managing capabilities. A CI-DR should be considered a transformational change to an information security or cybersecurity

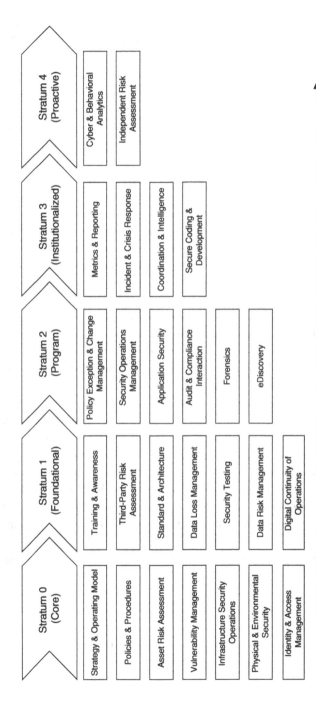

*Note: Capabilities can reside in either 1st Line or 2nd Line (2nd Line view preferred).
Additionally, capabilities may depend on risk appetites and/or size of company/geography.

FIGURE 4.1 CI-DR™ maturity.

program; going forward, the reader should consider the CI-DR program to be synonymous and interchangeable with a traditional information security or cybersecurity program. The first function that the CI-DR program has to develop or transform for it to become operational is the **governance** function. The governance function captures the capabilities and practices to consistently and cohesively operate a mature cybersecurity and risk management program. The CI-DR governance function must be able to oversee and govern its programs and have capabilities that create the interconnections and skeletal structure for this program to be successful. The next important function of CI-DR program is building or transforming an **information risk management** (IRM). The IRM program creates the necessary activities to ensure that risks to assets, which can be people, information, and information systems, are correctly assessed and aggregated and scored. The third function is the **security assurance** function, which is a critical component of a CI-DR program, as it determines the trustworthiness of information and information systems. The fourth function is simply called **security operations**, which comprises the conventional security engineering, oversight, and operational functions to build and maintain the protections to assets. Finally, the fifth function is **intelligence and response**. The intelligence and response function is where the analysis, collection, and dissemination of the CI-DR originates, and is where the program expands to include capabilities and practices focused on managing both proactive and reactive cyber events. This function also provides the early warning indicators, decision-support structures, and management of the cyber event and post-crisis activities. These five high-level functions set objectives for the capabilities within their scope, drive the embryonic matrix of connective tissues between capabilities, and provide the cellular-level information needed for the CI-DR program to create the "knowledge" or intelligence package designed for business leaders to make informed decisions about cyber risk.

Given now a high level of design for the functions, the CI-DR program cannot be executed without capabilities, and those capabilities must be able to meet a predefined set of objectives and answer a few high-level questions that can be expanded upon to meet organizational needs. The four capabilities within the **governance** function, strategy and operating model, policies and procedures, training and awareness, and metrics and reporting, are designed to address these types of questions. The **strategy and operating model** capability answers the following questions: Does your organization strategically align its cybersecurity goals with business and technology objectives? Is your cybersecurity program effectively operating to meet strategic business objectives? This capability is further separated into two sub-capabilities that are symbiotic to each other. One cannot meet the CI-DR strategy without designing, detailing, and driving how the program operates. Additionally, one cannot create an operating model without having strategic goals, objectives, and missions. After adequately setting and detailing how the CI-DR program operates, the program has to develop policies and procedures for each capability to meet the organization's objectives and the program's directions and objectives as defined in the previous chapter. The next capability with the governance function is **policies and procedures**, which are designed to answer the question: Are the CI-DR policies and procedures consistently executed enterprise-wide? Once policies and procedures have been implemented the **training and awareness** capability needs to follow and is inherently connected to policies and procedures as it sets the organization's culture, or the way in which leadership wants the rest of the organization to operate. A training and awareness capability answers the following question: Does the enterprise as a whole and each operating unit locally understand the cyber risks and what is expected from each employee, partner, vendor, or the third party using the company's information and information systems?

Training and awareness is often overlooked or is implemented to simply be a generic program without reiterating the policies it has created. There are many options for organizations to deploy this capability from lunch-and-learn events to online computer-based training, or by sponsoring various industry events. Additionally, many information technology and information/cybersecurity teams are often overlooked for training and are usually included in the generic training packages, instead of highly specialized training for their disciplines. The final capability under governance is **metrics and reporting**; this closes the interconnections within the governance function, but remains part of the embryonic matrix for other capabilities coming from the other CI-DR functions. Metrics and reporting is the heart of the overall program and answers the following questions: Has the CI-DR program identified the appropriate key risk indicators and key performance indicators (KRI/KPIs) for each functional capability? Has the CI-DR program identified important business and technology cyber risks? Are they presented with the right frequency, and does the audience understand the reports? Without metrics there is no ability to trend, set baselines, or show maturity; therefore, the reporting produced will not be about the decisions that need to be made.

We have defined our governance functions and capabilities; we can now build and mature the program through the **information risk management** (IRM) function. The IRM function has five capabilities that are interconnected within the IRM function and are part of the holistic embryonic matrix of connective tissue between the other CI-DR functional capabilities. We will explore that in further chapters and how the overall concept of building a CI-DR program works. The five capabilities in the IRM function are asset risk assessments, third-party risk assessments, policy exception and change management, audit and compliance interaction, and independent risk management. Any organization must know what their assets are, where they are located, and what is their importance or criticality to the way in which they operate and conduct business. The first capability for IRM is **asset risk assessments** and should be the starting place for knowing what assets are important for the organization and business. The asset risk assessment capability answers the following question: Are the organization's technology assets risk assessed consistently and conducted with conformity in each operating unit? This would include creating an asset's inherent risk profile, a criticality rating, the controls that ensure safe operations, and the residual risks after mitigations, controls, and processes have been implemented to reduce identified risks.

There are many assets today that are no longer within the organization's buildings, environments, or networks; the program addresses these possession issues through the **third-party risk assessments** capability. Third-party risk assessments support vendor management and procurement inside an organization by providing a consistent risk scoring prior to signing a contract with a vendor and through the vendor's contract with the organization. The third-party risk assessments capability is designed to answer the question, "Are all of the organization's third parties, partners, and vendors risk-assessed consistently and with conformity?" Risk management in any business unit needs to be able to treat and mitigate risks. The **policy exception and change management** capabilities enhance and ensure the CI-DR program is included if these functions are performed elsewhere within the organization. It is designed to answer the question, "Are exceptions to policy and changes to technology assets controlled, monitored, tracked, and appropriately reported in a consistent fashion across the enterprise?"

The final two capabilities within the IRM function that are valuable and create efficiency for an organization to address the amount of audit, compliance, and other third-party security requests are the audit and compliance interaction and independent risk management. The **audit and compliance interaction** capability provides operational efficiency for the number of requests for compliance and control effectiveness that an organization has to answer about cybersecurity. It provides clear, articulated, and consistent responses and answers the question, "Does the internal/external audit consistently validate and opine that the cybersecurity program is operating effectively and mitigating risks?" Finally, the CI-DR program leverages the **independent risk management** capability, which answers the questions, "Does the cybersecurity program effectively oversee business line technology risks?" "Do they provide proper oversight and have the correct mechanisms to elevate conflicts?" "What is the state of enterprise risk management, and does each operating unit effectively interact with independent risk management?"

Independent risk management capabilities have a long, storied, and disruptive past. The capability has been argued and debated about where it belongs and where it reports within an organization. I want to caution the reader: it should not matter whether this is considered a second line of assurance or something information technology risk testing is performing, first line. The key is that some part of the organization is performing self-assessments prior to external regulators, external auditors, or some cyber event putting the organization into a race to figure out what went wrong. Whoever in your organization is doing this, they must be independent of the IT organization, independent of the compliance department, and independent of the procurement or vendor management departments. If you are so small that you do not have the resources to do this within your organization, then put a budget aside and have an independent evaluator come and perform the testing and analysis. These do not have to be expensive if you are small with limited resources, but they will assist you as the business leadership to determine if you have some gaps in how your technology is deployed and what risks your organization might face in the future.

The **security assurance** function is more technical, provides the assurances for making the organization safe, and has five capabilities. Vulnerability management, standards and architecture, application security, data loss prevention, secure coding and development, and data risk management. **Vulnerability management** (VM) is the capability that proactively identifies, remediates, and reduces technical risks within the environment. VM, in this instance, focuses solely on infrastructure-type devices, such as servers, databases, endpoints, and network equipment. It is separate from application security due to the particular skills and tools needed to evaluate and maintain efficiency. The VM capability should answer the question, "Does the organization have an effective vulnerability management process that operates consistently across the enterprise?" Some organizations have business line–specific technology teams that are separate from the corporate or regional technology functions, and so it is important that the processes around VM are consistent. It also addresses the risk question, "Does my organization have any vulnerabilities that can be exploited to impact operations?" As VM is a key capability for this information, we will discuss this capability in another chapter.

The **standards and architecture** capability addresses the question, "Are technical standards consistent and complete across the enterprise?" Standards are what is created after a policy has been established and set the details and configurations for specific systems, devices, and encryption suites, which are all technical in nature. Many organizations mistakenly place standards within the policies, which makes them unreasonable to manage, too long to read, and stagnant, depending on the number of potential system or device standards trying to be forced into a policy. Additionally, many standards miss a security perspective. Architecture in a CI-DR program is differentiated from IT architecture, which has an operational or availability focus; consider this more of a security architecture capability. For example, a security architect might be involved in reviewing how the technology, not just security products, is placed, routed, or implemented within the organization. This is different from the infrastructure security operations under the security operations function. Without clear security architecture involved in both setting and implementing standards along with IT, the placement of systems and technologies within the organization's environment is already at risk.

The **application security** capability is differentiated from the security testing capability under security operations and is focused on similar activities as VM but requires differentiated skills, knowledge, and tools. This capability answers the question, "Does the organization have adequate and consistent application security practices and capabilities?" The **data loss prevention** capability is about managing, collecting, reporting, and preventing certain sensitive information from leaving the organization, or being accessed internally without authorization. The capability answers the question, "Is the organization aware of where its information is going, who is accessing it, and whether they have the authorization to do so?" The **secure coding and development** capability is an essential capability for any organization that provides internal or external development activities. It assists development teams internally and externally with a formal structure to support information, trends, and coding practices.

For example, if the organization is using an external development, this program creates the processes to ensure that the code received does not have backdoors, vulnerabilities, or Easter eggs embedded within the compiled code. Additionally, for internal development teams this capability provides for static and dynamic testing to identify vulnerability trends within a specific group or team, or of an individual. An example of a common trend identified is someone or some group continuing to generate cross-site scripting vulnerabilities within their code base. This capability would work with a development group or individual in providing the proper function, the proper code, or the necessary training to reduce this vulnerability trend. This capability also answers the questions, "Does the organization engage in internal development, or is this done externally?" and "How robust are the organization's secure coding and development practices internally, and do they hold their third parties accountable for safe coding practices?" The final capability within the security assurance function is **data risk management**, which is the capability that assists business units with defining sensitive information, compliance-type information, and other classifications. This capability answers the question, "Does the organization implement sufficient data management practices and capabilities?"

The **security operations** function consists of six capabilities: idenity and access management, security operations management, infrastructure security operations, security testing, physical and environmental security, and digital continuity of operations. These capabilities are designed to provide oversight, sometimes operations, and assurances of the operating components and infrastructure of the organization's security technologies and protection mechanisms. This function is both technical and operational in design and assists all operational processes in the organization by ensuring risks and security mechanisms are identified and operating effectively. The **identity and access management** capability goes further than the traditional provisioning usually completed by the IT department. The capability addresses the following questions, "Does the organization operate effective and consistent identity and access management functions?"and "Are roles and access levels defined and monitored, and are violations reported in a timely manner?" Different organizations can have this function as a supportive capability, an oversight capability, or as the primary capability for dealing with the asset class of people.

The **security operations management** capability is the management, monitoring, collection, and interaction with the organization's security operations center (SOC) or managed security service provider (MSSP). Either the SOC or the MSSP is typically the central location for all infrastructure security tools to report into, either by sending logs or by using machine learning to identify anomalous data or provide a wide range of threat intelligence, or security testing capabilities. This capability addresses the questions, "Does the organization have an active security operations center?"and "Is the organization able to identify anomalous activity within the organization?" The

infrastructure security operations capability is designed specifically to be responsible for the organization's security tools. This is another capability where it can be argued or debated where this capability resides. The capability addresses the questions, "Does the organization operate an effective and consistent infrastructure security program?" and "Does the organization have the appropriate technical protection mechanisms in place across the enterprise?"

The **security testing** capability is operational in nature and different from VM or application security. This capability informs the organization whether the controls implemented were effective, identifies whether vulnerabilities were properly remediated, or changes the prioritization of risk. It is also responsible for scoping, targeting, and scheduling testing whether done internally or by external third parties. This capability answers the question, "Has the organization effectively prioritized and mitigated technology, facility, and people risks?" Penetration testing, as many readers will know, is only a small percentage of the testing that needs to be done. The term "Red Team" is a better fit for truly performing the task to answer the question. In addition to security testing the organization needs to have **physical and environmental security** capabilities. This capability tests, monitors, and remediates risks to the organization's physical security such as ingress and egress points, badge access, visitor access, and access to building environmental utilities. There are numerous news articles on how malware entered the organization's digital operational environments through interconnected networks that should have been logically or physically separated. The capability answers the question, "Does the organization have physical and environmental security policies and procedures that are consistent across the organization and its locations?"

The last capability under security operations is **digital continuity of operations**. This terminology is closely related to military continuity of operations planning (COOP) and has similar characteristics. This capability covers CI-DR needs for business continuity planning (BCP) and IT disaster recovery (DR) activities. There are needs such as physical security at colocation facilities and hot-site locations for BCP. Imagine going through all the exercise and planning on moving the majority of employees to another location only to find that the location is not safe; it allows individuals from other organizations to roam and access your organization's new location, not safe at all. Additionally, for DR exercises there have been numerous times that I have been a part of monitoring, observing, or consulting organizations during their DR activities, only to find that they left security out to get the systems up and running. This places the organization directly at risk, as the systems, applications, and data are open to anyone because the controls were not properly implemented at startup time. The capability addresses the question, "Does the organization have an industry-standard business continuity/disaster recovery program?"

Intelligence and response is the fifth and final function for the CI-DR program. This is the key location where the intelligence lifecycle rotation lives. The intelligence and response function has five capabilities, incident and crisis response, coordination and intelligence, cyber behavioral analytics, forensics, and eDiscovery. **Incident and crisis response** is the process and design of how a cybersecurity event becomes escalated to an incident and from an incident to a crisis. As described in the Preface to this book, an event, given its magnitude, velocity, and impact, can quickly become a crisis for an organization. The most important part is that the cyber playbooks and escalation processes meet the organization's crisis management operations. If not aligned, an organization can become paralyzed attempting to figure out who needs to be involved, who is leading which section, and key decisions will be missed or not communicated effectively. This capability answers the questions, "Does the organization have effective incident/crisis response planning?" and "How often does the organization perform cyber stress testing scenarios?" Cyber stress testing is very similar to how an organization does financial or market stress testing. Scenarios are developed, tested, and lessons learned are incorporated back into the process. The **coordination and intelligence** capability is the lifeblood and resource program where CI-DR gathers its "knowledge" and performs its analysis from.

The capability provides for intelligence analysts, drives the fusion center program, and follows the intelligence life cycle of answering critical intelligence requirements (CIRs) or priority intelligence requirements (PIRs) from business leadership. It is also the capability where the traditional Cyber Threat Intelligence program resides and collaborates with the other key parts of the CI-DR program. Those interconnections or "connective tissue," as we refer to them, will be discussed in the next chapter. This capability answers the question, "Does the organization have a sufficient cyber threat intelligence program?" **Forensics and eDiscovery** capabilities allow for the organization to perform internal network and system forensics, reverse malware engineering, and litigation requests. The skills in the capability are different from traditional information security or cybersecurity professionals, due to the legal requirements of evidence collection and chain-of-custody specifications for digital transfer of data. The capability also has a set of tools that are unique that can assist an organization internally to ensure information is not leaked externally or that the organization decides not to involve law enforcement and keep the matter internally. These capabilities answer the question, "Does the organization have access to the necessary forensic capabilities should they be needed?" The final capabilities within this function are **cyber and behavioral analytics**. These capabilities are designed for organizations with more maturity in their CI-DR programs.

The common question that I find throughout conversations and engagements with different organizations is, "Now that you have told me all of this, where do I start?" To start, organizations need to check and return to the basics, looking at how your cyber strategy aligns with business, what are the most critical assets and how you are protecting them, starting from the physical and moving to the logical, and ending with the ability to adapt and pivot as the business moves and grows. The framework shown in Figure 4.2 has taken me years to adapt, test, execute, and refresh. Each of the connective capabilities are building blocks that without having at least some maturity in each capability the next stratum level capabilities are not able to operate.

When we discuss cyber analytics, we mean the intelligence that is gathered from open source, closed sources, vulnerability management, security and application testing, and specific data from the security operations center. This is the deep analytics that should be built with machine learning capabilities, and other techniques needed to harness the amount and specific requests (CIRs or PIRs) that can be automated. Behavioral analytics cannot be done without clean identities and access management processes. Additionally, it could take into account the data risk assessments and assets risk assessments to determine whether an individual or machine should have access to a specific file, folder, or data element. It answers the question, "Is the organization sufficiently invested in the technical capabilities and practices necessary to detect and report on anomalous behaviors?"

Additional impressions and observations that can be answered through the CI-DR program are about leadership and risk culture. The questions that the CI-DR program answers around leadership are "Does executive management in each operating unit display commitment, direction, and support to cybersecurity efforts (i.e. tone at the top)?" "Is the 'Head of Information Security' in the correct reporting structure?" "Does the role have the appropriate levels of authority?" Additionally, it answers the questions for the organization's risk culture, such as "Does the risk culture in each operating unit support enterprise cybersecurity objectives?" "Do they provide for the integration of cybersecurity risks?"

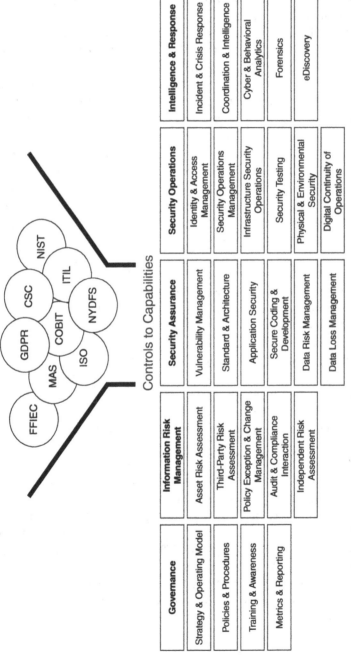

FIGURE 4.2 CI-DR™ functions and capabilities.

NOTES

- CI-DR programs cannot operate in silos; they must be a part of the information security program, a business intelligence and fraud program, and must be directly able to communicate and respond to any business leader's request for cyber information.
- Foundations are important; they must be simply defined and designed to answer critical questions posed by the industry and the risks, regulators, or legislation that impact operations or objectives for the organization.
- Capabilities are also important to be designed and defined to ensure individuals have the skills necessary to make each capability effective. The NIST NICE[1] is a good reference for particular skill sets needed to accomplish each capability. It is a good reference to start with for organizations looking to identify quality people for each capability.

---

[1] William Newhouse, Stephanie Keith, National Initiative for Cybersecurity Education (NICE) Cybersecurity Workforce Framework, US Department of Commerce, https://doi.org/10.6028/NIST.SP.800-181.

CHAPTER FIVE

Functional Capabilities of the CI-DR™ Program

Pursue one great decisive aim with force and determination.

– Carl von Clausewitz

THIS CHAPTER continues the discussion from the previous chapter about the functions and capabilities needed to make the CI-DR™ efficient, operational, and adaptive to the demands of a cyber and operational risk program. This chapter will discuss how each of the capabilities identified above interoperate through what we call "connective tissue" and show the value of removing silos and boundaries for maximum effectiveness.

Again, we begin this chapter with real-life examples to show the need for the embryonic CI-DR matrix and connective tissue requirements and how they can benefit the business leader. Reports that come to executives around cybersecurity always have some number of vulnerabilities in the ecosystem. However, there are a few organizations that have moved from just pure numbers to show trending information, which is a good beginning in maturing a cybersecurity program, but trending information still has no decision points that can be easily discerned from this type of reporting. Figure 5.3 is an example of reporting I see consistently across many organizations. The report shown at the least identifies that patching and vulnerabilities are not being consistently applied. The reason this company is not mitigating risk could be from a combination of issues:

- The company does not have a robust patching and vulnerability management (VM) program.
- The company does not allocate resources to perform the activity.
- The systems have been considered critical and therefore cannot be restarted after patches or vulnerabilities have been fixed.
- The business units have not identified maintenance times to allow the systems to be restarted.
- The company does not think that vulnerabilities are important enough to fix due to operational needs.
- The company does not have a robust disaster recovery or redundant failover systems to be able to perform the testing, remediation, and restarting for systems.

Each of the items listed for reasons why an organization is not fixing their systems is a direct result of not providing business leaders with options and decision points on fixing systems and the criticality of doing so. This is exactly why the CI-DR embryonic matrix was created to establish the "story" with "knowledge" so that business leaders directly understand the operational impacts and risks associated with not performing basic cyber hygiene and maintenance. The CI-DR program is responsible for planning and direction, the collection of information, processes, and potentially uses exploitation methods to determine feasibility, performs the analysis and production of reporting, and disseminates the report for consumption by business leadership and other stakeholders. See Figure 2.1 in Chapter 2 for a refresh on the CI-DR intelligence life cycle. Starting with this critical example, the question "What is the most critical activity we need to perform to reduce the risk of exposure or business interruption in our systems?" is answered.

The CI-DR process, as we have mentioned, needs to be cyclic in nature. That cyclic nature has to be processed through the requirements sent from the Executive Team, as in Figure 5.1 we can begin to set expectations for reporting, risk, and direction by understanding the "connective tissue" between capabilities to obtain the appropriate direction for our example above. To demonstrate,

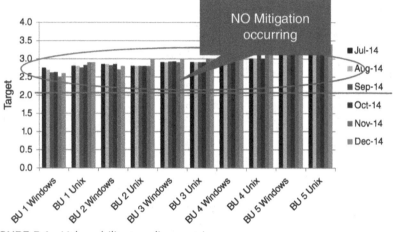

FIGURE 5.1 Vulnerability trending metrics.

let's start with those CIRs and PIRs we have listed in Figure 3.1 in Chapter 3. The CI-DR program starts in the Coordination and Intelligence capability, for collecting data. The collections from the Asset Risk Assessment capability begin with what are the organization's "crown jewels" and most risky technology assets. The Asset Risk Assessment program would pass along information similar to the following:

- Location of Asset (Internal, External, DMZ, Hosted)
- Information Sensitivity – highest classified level of information, i.e., Public, Internal, Confidential, etc. (This would come from the Data Risk Management Categorization.)
- PHI (Yes/No), important from a regulatory loss perspective
- PII (Yes/No), important from a regulatory loss perspective
- Number of PHI records – helps to quantify potential loss due to regulatory fines from breach
- Number of PII records – helps to quantify potential loss due to regulatory fines from breach
- Payment Application (Yes/No) – important based on regulations, and potential ability to recapture loss based on type, i.e. SWIFT, WIRE, ACH, etc.
- RTO/RPO rating – goes to validate the availability loss impact

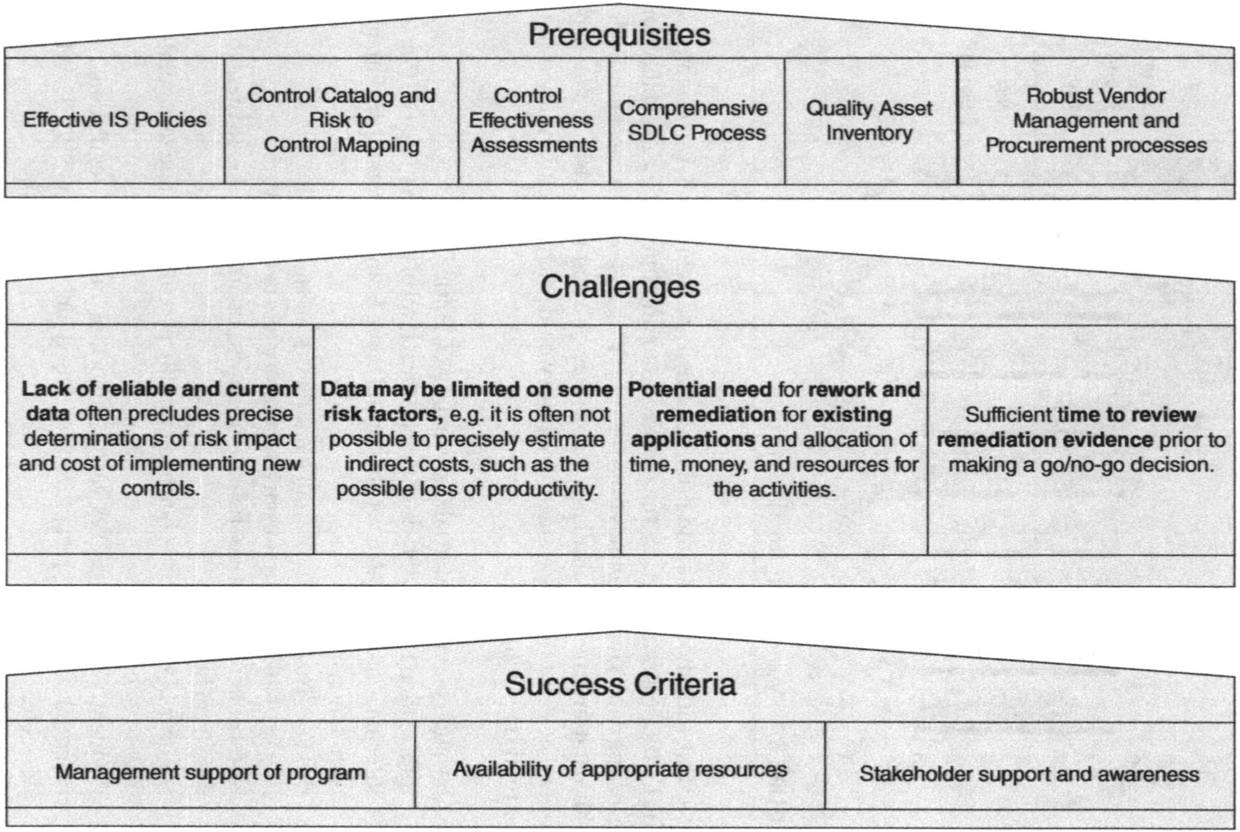

Prerequisites

| Effective IS Policies | Control Catalog and Risk to Control Mapping | Control Effectiveness Assessments | Comprehensive SDLC Process | Quality Asset Inventory | Robust Vendor Management and Procurement processes |

Challenges

Lack of reliable and current data often precludes precise determinations of risk impact and cost of implementing new controls.

Data may be limited on some risk factors, e.g. it is often not possible to precisely estimate indirect costs, such as the possible loss of productivity.

Potential need for rework and remediation for existing applications and allocation of time, money, and resources for the activities.

Sufficient time to review remediation evidence prior to making a go/no-go decision.

Success Criteria

| Management support of program | Availability of appropriate resources | Stakeholder support and awareness |

FIGURE 5.2 Risk and control success.

- Audit or Compliance identified critical rated application (Yes/No) – important in the event there are already action plans and remediation efforts ongoing
- Third-Party Risk Score – what is the vendor's security score that is hosting the asset and data?

While this is not an exhaustive list, it provides for the first step in moving toward classifying an asset (Figure 5.2). You can have more data or less data, but it will need to include many of these data elements.

From the list above there four different capabilities mentioned within these bullets, with asset risk assessments, data risk management, audit and compliance interaction, and third-party risk assessments contributing to the collection for any one particular asset. This provides that ability for an organization to identify inherent risk, asset criticality, and residual risks. Figure 5.3 shows the process of asset risks.

Using the process in Figure 5.3 and data elements from asset risk assessments, third-party risk assessments, and audit and compliance, that information is connected to secure coding and development activities, data risk assessments, and standards and architecture (Figure 5.4). Secure coding and development uses information about the assets, system, platform, code language, and application types to write code and configuration requirements on how the assets will be used by end users or other systems or applications through various programming interfaces. Any asset must have data to work and interoperate with end users or other systems or applications, and so data risk assessments help developers, system administrators, risk managers, and business leaders understand the sensitivity of the data. As sensitivity increases, i.e. becomes more valuable to the organization, different techniques, standards, and architecture are necessary to make them safe. We can under-stand the importance of why the standards and architecture capability is a primary capability of information from other capabilities and disseminator of information into other connective capabilities.

The information and output from the secure coding and development, data risk assessments, and standards and architecture disseminates data and information to the infrastructure security operations, identity and access management, and physical and environmental capabilities. The information transferred to these three capabilities allows for access to be appropriately granted, based on the asset's location and use and the data sensitivity. It also takes into consideration that the controls are about protection, like colocation access, the organization's owned data centers, and how access is controlled, or

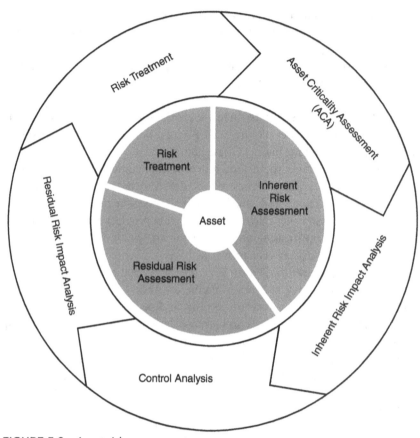

FIGURE 5.3 Asset risk assessment.

cloud-hosted environments – each have their own requirements. Infrastructure operations also has to take the information being processed about what tools or network protocols may need to be evaluated for how the assets interact. Again, these three capabilities share cyclic information; as infrastructure and physical security information change the way in which the other operates, so does the access and identification of users need to adjust in permissions. As we mentioned, the data risk assessments are important to understand the value of data to the organization, and they are also monitored through the data loss pevention capability. The data and information collected from these capabilities are sent to the security operations management capability for monitoring and alerting should the various configurations, access, and

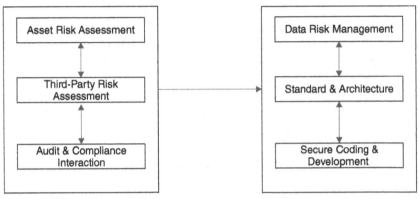

FIGURE 5.4 Assets to architecture.

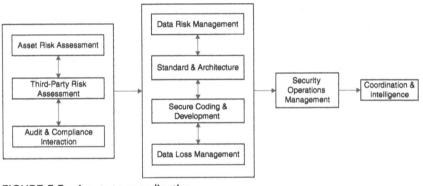

FIGURE 5.5 Assets to coordination.

other key data be out of specifications with standards and benchmarks (Figure 5.5). The security operations management process is the central area for the majority of collections and we will discuss a component of this capability in Chapter 6.

Once the assets are established and the environment and infrastructure is designed appropriately, the monitoring of the asset's vulnerabilities and testing of controls capabilities begin to examine whether the other capabilities are operating effectively. The next area that would send information into the CI-DR collections process is from the VM capability and information forwarded is about specific assets and their identified vulnerabilities from automated scanning tools. The VM key data points would be the CVSS[1] scoring and the CVE[2] information. Upon receipt into the collection process the CVSS scoring needs to be validated to ensure the temporal and environmental scores match to the asset's criticality scoring (i.e. inherent risk, residual risk). By validating during the analysis phase the organization can provide feedback to various groups conducting asset risk scoring, and level-set anything that is out of standard or misaligned. A CVE provides known vulnerabilities that exist in operating systems, network devices, applications, and other utilities and protocols. We will discuss the VM program in more detail in the upcoming dedicated chapter. The VM process is also cyclic in nature in that information and remediation efforts in near-real-time are valuable to the organization, as it would constantly adjust the risk levels per asset. There is an obvious need to ensure that the CI-DR collection and analysis process have the ability to consistently have the scoring updated.

The application security capability is also necessary to feed information into the CI-DR collections process. Applications vulnerabilities similar to infrastructure vulnerabilities are important to determine the risk levels for an asset. Most if not all applications require infrastructure and certain configurations to operate, and therefore are connected together from an overall system-to-platform-to-application perspective. Many vulnerabilities for applications can be introduced by the system or platform itself, inviting techniques to circumvent application protections. As we mentioned previously, applications within organizations are varied in type, which is why this specific capability is differentiated from VM, but not the process. The variety of applications can come as mobile applications, web applications, web services, desktop applications, embedded applications, console applications, etc., all of which would require different tools and skills to assess issues in code languages and platforms. Information that is forwarded and reported may leverage something similar to application threat classifications, as shown in Figure 5.6. The classification of this data is standardized across multiple types of hardware and software through the CWE[3] scoring system.

Vulnerability management, application security, and the security operations management capabilities additionally connect to the security testing capability to assist in targeting or scoping what assets need to have a closer look to determine whether a vulnerability can be exploited and access to data

---

[1] National Institute of Technology and Standards, Common Vulnerability Scoring System v3, https://nvd.nist.gov/vuln-metrics/cvss/v3-calculator.

[2] Mitre, Common Vulnerabilities and Exposures, 2020, https://cve.mitre.org/.

[3] Mitre, Common Weakness Enumeration,2020, https://cwe.mitre.org/about/index.html.

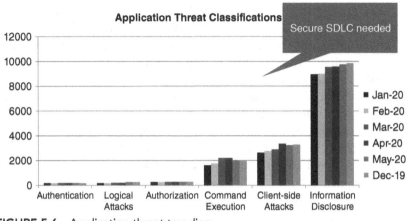

FIGURE 5.6 Application threat trending.

is compromised. Security testing is a key component and is included in the collections chapter of this book and identifies quickly what to look for and how to properly scope the tests to reduce cost, answer key CIRs or PIRs, and to provide the CI-DR program with valuable threat information during the analysis phase. Security testing provides the CI-DR processing and exploitation phase to understand where faults reside within the organization and can create appropriate options for a business leader's decision. Security testing is a key function and there have been a ton of books and process documents that we briefly mentioned in the collections chapter of this book for deeper understanding of how an organization can reduce costs, create better efficiency, and mitigate real threats to the organization. Forensic information from breach remediation, reverse malware analysis, and trending information from litigation can also be leveraged to support the security testing capability and the dissemination of knowledge from the coordination and intelligence capability can be connected back to the forensic team, specifically if in post-breach containment efforts on where and what systems to focus one's efforts. Forensics is another capability that has a dedicated chapter to show the value of this overlooked capability (Chapter 8).

▪ Cyber and behavioral analytics capabilities enter the embryonic matrix through data received from the identity and access management capability, the infrastructure security, and the physical and environmental capability. The identity and access management provides the cyber and behavioral with data regarding identifying specific individuals with accounts or usernames, the specific roles the individual has within the organization, and their access levels to different systems and applications to determine "patterns of life" during their day-to-day job activities. The analytics from this capability also has a direct impact and risk-adjusting scoring to an organization, as its purpose is to look for activities such as:

- Insider theft or destruction
- Constrained network bandwidth and computer resources
- Inability to identify a sophisticated cyberattack
- Inefficient incident response to lateral movement
- Regulatory fines
- Customer fraud
- Inability to protect personally identifiable information (PII) and critical resources (data, cryptographic keys, systems, etc.)

For example, if Bob, who is an accountant and works in the Finance Department, usually badges into the facility at 0800 and leaves daily at 1800, that specific information may be one of the data elements from the Physical and Environmental Security capability. Additionally, if every day Bob logs into the bob_user account and accesses the ERP system, and then accesses a particular spreadsheet on the organization's shared document platform, those additional data points can be valuable in determining the working pattern for Bob. Should Bob open a sensitive file that was not authorized through the role or access, and send that file to his home email, the cyber and behavioral capability would raise an alert. This type of information can then be used in the coordination and intelligence capability for preemptive notification to business leaders that there is a potential breach. That breach could impact the organization through litigation, regulations, or internal processes where the forensic capability would have specific information on where to begin their collection of information for whichever consequence the data loss created.

The metrics and reporting capability has the responsibility for producing reports for various stakeholders within the organization and allows the CI-DR program to leverage the different reporting requirements to create additional "knowledge" for decisions. Additionally, this capability is responsible for setting, maintaining, and supporting the metrics from each capability in the CI-DR program, providing key skill sets, oversight of key information needed, such as key risk indicators (KRIs) and key performance indicators (KPIs), and integrating with other reporting functions within the organization. For example, the cyber-security leadership may need data on how the Department is operating and areas within the organization that may be deficient from a security perspective. The risk and compliance leadership may only need to know what controls are failing and if those controls have an impact on fines from regulations, failure to meet service level agreements (SLAs), or from business interruptions. The technology leaders may only need to have a report that shows the effectiveness of their patching, change management, configuration management, secure development activities, and whether architecture designs are meeting security expectations and controls. All these types of reports for stakeholders can be combined and leveraged to support decision areas where the business leadership may want to address a particular risk or understand where resources may have to be diverted. Metrics and reporting is also connected with the CI-DR program into the training and awareness capability, the policies and procedures capability, the strategy and operating model capability, and the digital continuity of operations capability.

Training and awareness has a direct impact from the metrics and reporting. For example, if the Learning Management System (LMS) identifies that employees are not doing well for phishing tests, or that the development teams are still coding with embedded issues, this capability can put forth courses, trainings, or lunch-and-learns to address the risks that are being raised from metrics. Additionally, if it was determined through training that employees still may not understand a particular policy or procedure, or if it was identified that the process was incorrectly captured as a workflow, then the training and awareness capability can have an impact on changing and modifying existing policies, or create new ones, to address those risks. Training and awareness capabilities are mostly low-cost efforts to support executive management's culture, guidance, or "tone from the top" directions. Most security training programs for employees are stagnant and do not set aside specific training for technologists or other specialized employees. This is where training can be most effective and have a positive impact on how the organization views security, and the value that an individual has within the organization to protect the organization.

Policies and procedures can be created specific enough through conducting interviews, understanding how the organization works, and from leveraging the International Standards Organization's 27000 series (ISO 27000) to create the necessary security policies. What is missing, however, is the applicability of those policies and consistent execution. Policies and procedures can only be fine-tuned through testing, either by internal or external assessments. Additionally, metrics plays a massive role in determining the effectiveness and consistent execution of policies and procedures. Those

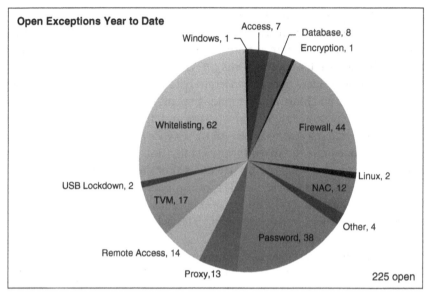

FIGURE 5.7   Exception trending.

metrics can come through capabilities such as policy exceptions, security testing, incident management After Action Reports (AARs), or training failures for particular subjects. Obviously, policy exception and change management are instruments for ensuring that the organization is following its policies and procedures and allows for the CI-DR program to be engaged with changes, and raise concerns if changes do not address risks or if changes increase risks. Figure 5.7 identified through metrics that password exceptions, firewall rules, and whitelisting are areas that needed review. Through careful reviews and scrutinous technical reviews these metrics provided the organization the ability to adapt and modify policies and procedures to lower the amount of exceptions. Additionally, these metrics were able to focus on some technology standards that had to be adjusted or new ones created.

The strategy and operating model has connective tissue to the metrics and reporting, training and awareness, and policies and procedures capabilities. Strategy in the modern cyber age can no longer be static for the timelines most organizations set (i.e. 3–5 years); it must be adaptable to take on new challenges the business or industry demands. A strategy is easily adaptable with a CI-DR program providing the "knowledge," decision structures, and options to address business requirements and needs. Many security strategies increase personnel due to increasing the number of silos and tools that do not interact and provide the value needed to create the operational risk and executive CIRs needed to properly address the organization's objectives. I am not saying that tools are the culprit for increase in complexity, but I have observed organizations "following the herd" and buying tools that are not necessary, or solving the risk concerns of another organization. You, as the reader, should judge if you have disparate tools and silos that should be working for the benefit of the business.

Metrics and reporting's connective tissue also sends "knowledge" to the digital continuity of operations capability, which can then send "knowledge" to the incident and crisis management capability. The metrics that are generated and reports created by the CI-DR program provide input to the digital continuity of operations capability by informing that area of assets where criticality has changed and if there are risks that are not addressed or have to be addressed, depending on the DR or BCP program's interdependency of assets. For example, new information was identified that an asset is now responsible for hosting the organization's sensitive data (e.g. organization moves from on-premises Share-Point to Azure SharePoint or from Director's Desk to a different platform, etc.). If the organization is not running a traditional "Hot Site" as in fully replicated systems, then the DR program could bring up the incorrect platform or systems without the access controls, or data links necessary to continue proper operations. Any failure in operations is a cost to the organization, which it does not account for in its risk structures. A CI-DR program addresses these concerns by identifying them, holding accountable the proper owner, and reporting them in the dissemination activities.

Digital continuity of operations is then connected to the incident and crisis management capability, by providing that incoming "knowledge" from the metrics and reporting capability and sending any updates and changes so that the organization can appropriately recover in the event of an incident or crisis. As mentioned, After Action Reports and lessons learned, whether through Tabletop Exercises (TTX) or actual incidents or crises, feed back into the cycle of the CI-DR program's Coordination and Intelligence capability. The ability to interconnect and be a valuable instrument for crisis management assists the organization when in crisis mode and contributes cyber to the leadership team, and ensures that cyber, as the most critical operational risk today, is in lockstep with the leadership and other people running the crisis management process. The industry talks about ways to make cyber a part of the organization; contributing to, and being an instrument for, crisis management is one such way that cyber can get a seat at the table and be a collaborative program for leaders in making decisions.

Business leaders need to understand the connective tissue between all the capabilities in the CI-DR program in the same way that market risk impacts ratings, which impacts customers, which impacts revenue. Similarly, business leaders understand the Monte Carlo scenarios working for figuring out capital and liquidity risks. The CI-DR program simply provides the overall connective nature of how cyber "knowledge" can play a role in business decisions. Some articles or industry professionals may call the flow simply from assets to vulnerabilities to threats, which is not wrong; it just doesn't explain how to execute that solution. In this book we call it the "connective tissue".

NOTES

- Every CI-DR capability is interconnected to another capability through an embryonic matrix called "connective tissue."
- Each CI-DR capability provides metrics to other capabilities.
- The connective tissue between the capabilities and the ability to collect, analyze, and disseminate the information as "knowledge" should be focused on business leadership decisions and requirements.
- Silos are an organizational killer and, if not addressed, then the "black box" technical jargon becomes the obstacle for business leaders in understanding cyber risks.
- Cyber risk cannot be identified or solved by technology alone; there has to be a fusion or collaborative effort between a security function, a technology function, and a business function.
- Organizations are able to determine a profile that best describes them, either by indications of targeted attacks or by cyber footprint.
- Organizations starting a new cyber intelligence function are able to identify/craft the objective for the function.
- Organizations are able to utilize the guidance on key competencies, skills, and traits of an intelligence analyst to craft job descriptions and hire analysts needed to support the cyber intelligence function.
- Organizations are able to utilize the guidance on leadership to identify and hire the best person to lead the cyber intelligence function.
- Organizations are able to utilize the guidance on analyst experience and tools and technical proficiencies to identify the most competent staff and the tools needed to support successful analysis.
- Organizations are able to determine the progression path of their cyber intelligence function and use the guidance provided to identify the leadership experience, analyst experience, tools, and technical proficiencies to advance their cyber intelligence capabilities.

CHAPTER SIX

CI-DR™ Key Capability Next-Generation Security Operations Center

To be practical, any plan must take account of the enemy's power to frustrate it.

Carl von Clausewitz, Prussian general

Introduction by Kiran Vangaveti – CEO of BluSapphire

In today's world of ever-faster-paced evolution and adoption of technology, businesses big or small have to adapt and protect their intellectual property (IP) along with sensitive information about their customers, partners, employees, and operations. Chances of a breach have risen substantially, and the odds of a breach are high. With these threats in mind, more and more businesses are turning toward a security operations center (SOC) to help them prevent, identify, and defend themselves against these threats.

Security operation centers (SOC) are generally defined as teams of expert facility whose members dedicate themselves entirely to information security operations. These individuals use a range of computer programs and specialized security processes that can pinpoint weaknesses in the company's infrastructure and prevent these vulnerabilities from leading to a breach.

(continued)

(*continued*)

SIEM tools have generally been at the center of every traditional SOC. A SIEM tool collects logs from multiple sources and matches them against a specific ruleset that has been defined by an SOC and alerts the analysts if there is a match. These alerts are picked up by SOC analysts who proceed to perform a triage on the incident and take appropriate actions, often labeled as Response. This is often a reactive approach. An SOC's efficiency is also often measured on mean-time-to-respond. However, as the size and complexity of the IT environment increases, these analysts are often overburdened with alerts and the triage functions leading to alert fatigue. This often leads to expensive mistakes that often result in a breach going undetected, a total failure of the fundamental reason for an SOC's existence.

The evolving and escalating threat environment and the shift in security defense from prevention to a balance of prevention, detection, and response have prompted a renewed adoption of SOCs by a wider user base. The goal is to focus on the detection, response, and prevention of security incidents and threats, and to become continuously adaptive via newer capabilities in security analytics, use of threat intelligence (TI), and automation. This is achieved by using a combination of technologies that provide telemetry across data centers, networks, endpoints, users, and cloud. Next-gen SOCs move beyond the preventive technologies such as firewalls, IDS, IPS, and anti-virus and utilize a broader technology stack that enables security telemetry gathering, analysis, and incident management capabilities. Endpoint detection and response (EDR), network traffic analysis (NTA), and security orchestration automation and response (SOAR) are some common technologies that have started to enable next-gen SOCs with the arsenal needed.

Next-gen security operation centers (SOCs) are able to disrupt an attacker's threat life cycle and contain an incident, as opposed to the ad-hoc reactive approach of traditional SOCs. Next-gen SOC focuses on the following:

- High-fidelity threat detection and validation of attacks that have bypassed existing security controls.
- Use of a combination of technologies like network traffic analysis (NTA), endpoint activity monitoring, behavior analysis, sandbox analysis, deception and threat hunting.
- Proactive detection of threats using a combination of threat hunting and threat intelligence.
- Faster detection of threats.

- Faster triage of incidents.
- Faster response leveraging automation (i.e. quarantining the endpoint, blocking IP address on IPS or firewall, etc.).

As architected over the previous chapters, each CI-DR™ function has at least five capabilities, and those capabilities are interconnected by the embryonic matrix we call "connective tissue." We chose to focus this chapter on only the SOC capabilities, as it is the epicenter of data and the information collected is used to turn intelligence information from cyber data points into "knowledge" used for business decisions. In this chapter we will discuss and identify what most organizations are paying for today and why it is ineffective and costly. Most business leaders hardly ever get valuable information from the SOC except when there is an incident due to misconfigurations, tools only capable of handling certain types of information, or the tools and dependent tools only being able to follow a sequential set of rules and that skip or miss key events on which to alert. We will discuss this further in this chapter.

An SOC works a bit differently from a network operations center (NOC). An NOC is primarily responsible for system and infrastructure availability, as well as configuration and care and maintenance of digital and electronic assets. Because the NOC is responsible for availability, there are specific nuances that the SOC collects, which also can be operational in nature. For example, the SOC may find through analysis that a particular application is communicating ineffectively and causing system events to think there is an attack. The SOC can therefore provide recommendations to the NOC and development teams on how to fix the code or configurations to work more effectively in the organization's environment. The usages that an SOC can perform should be evaluated and move from traditional to integrated and useful.

As architected in the CI-DR program, the SOC is the CI-DR capability that deals with security information either at a strategic or tactical level; it is the epicenter of intelligence information becoming knowledge for the CI-DR program. Our vision of the SOC's capabilities aligns with the NIST definition of Information Security Continuous Monitoring: "Maintaining ongoing awareness of information security, vulnerabilities, and threats to support organizational risk management decisions."[1] However, a majority of organizations are only using their SOC at the tactical level, whether this is due

---

[1] Kelley Dempsey, Victoria Yan Pillitteri, *Assessing Information Security Continuous Monitoring Programs*, NIST SP 800-137, https://doi.org/10.6028/NIST.SP.800-137A.

to costs, a lack of understanding of what is out there in regard to tools and abilities, or lack of skills, both at the SOC and at the organization. In keeping with this book's real-world experiences, most tactical-level SOCs that I have deployed over the years have a simple hierarchy comprising the following components:

1. Log-collector tool
2. Local or remote security incident and event management (SIEM) tool
3. A bridge-head forwarder to send logs to offsite locations
4. A log retention tool
5. Analysts
6. Dashboard or alert functions
7. A ticket system

Additionally, by design and definition, an SOC can be also used for either physical or digital environments, operated by analysts with a subject-matter specialty and based on a 24-hour-day duty cycle, provided through shift-type work periods. An important note to remember throughout this book is that an SOC is not a command center and should not be considered one, nor as the location at which organizational decisions are made. The term *cyber SOC* has been around for a few decades, being derived from a 1998 Presidential Decision Directive, NSC-63,[2] which called for the creation of critical infrastructure protection and the warning and information centers.

While this author did not identify when the first usage of the term *SOC* was used, it is not listed in the National Information Assurance Glossary in 2010,[3] but can be purposed from the concepts of Computer Network Defense and Information Operations.

For our purposes, we will be discussing a cyber SOC that deals with both cybersecurity and cyber intelligence disciplines or, as you read above, next-generation SOC. When I purchased and began running and operating my information security program with an SOC in 2009, their goal was to collect and analyze security event logs from network devices and host systems and assist the organization in responding to sequential alerts and incidents. Years later, the SOC expanded from basic security event collections and analysis to operating more as what could be considered a managed security

---

[2] US Government, Presidential Decision Directive NSC/63, White House 1998, https://fas.org/irp/offdocs/pdd/pdd-63.htm.
[3] Committee on National Security Systems, CNSS Instruction No. 4009, 2010, https://www.hsdl.org/?abstract&did=7447.

service provider (MSSP) by including other cybersecurity devices, technology, and other relevant security data. An MSSP is defined as an organization's cybersecurity capabilities (core or advanced) and may, in some cases, be implemented and maintained by an MSSP. An organization may use an MSSP to provide capabilities that cannot be practically or cost-effectively developed in-house. MSSPs offer a variety of cybersecurity services and expertise that can be used to augment and enhance an organization's security capabilities. There are many approaches to using MSSPs, and the degree to which an organization depends on an MSSP for their information sharing and incident coordination varies. Some organizations may choose to outsource all cyber-security operations while others only specific components or capabilities. Small to medium-sized organizations may use an MSSP or a turnkey solution when the personnel and skills necessary to perform a task are not readily available within the organization, or in cases where the desired services can be provided by an MSSP at a lower cost. When selecting an MSSP, the following factors should be considered:

- The MSSP should be engaged with information-sharing communities and have ready access to actionable threat intelligence.[4]
- The MSSP service level agreement (SLA) should clearly describe the responsibilities of the parties entering into the agreement and establish a dynamic, adaptive cybersecurity strategy that utilizes information received from both internal and external sources.
- An organization that relies on an MSSP to provide some portion of its cybersecurity operations needs to integrate the MSSP-provided capabilities with the organization's internal cybersecurity capabilities and support the exchange of threat intelligence between the organization and the MSSP.

The SOC in the CI-DR program is the central collections of all events, data metrics, and logs that can contribute to the safety and soundness of the organization. Therefore, the SOC is one of the most important and valuable capabilities for the organization to properly leverage the CI-DR framework and programs. Business leaders should ask their technology and security leaders about the type of SOC the company has or is looking to purchase; the decisions that will be derived from the SOC's analysis impacts how business leadership makes decisions and is what a stakeholder should be asking.

---

[4] Chris Johnson, Lee Badger, *Guide to Cyber Threat Information Sharing*, NIST SP 800 – 150, http://dx.doi.org/10.6028/NIST.SP.800-150.

Another key requirement for an SOC is to allow modularity of tools that can be consumed into its repository. Any decision on purchasing an SOC should leverage industry standards or new standards that will accept legacy protocols or standards. A good example here is how elastic search and other similar technologies have the ability to sift through differently formatted logs to find the events it needs. These tools can ingest legacy, new, or sometimes custom exported data feeds to make searching and analysis easier. The final part of modularity should include capabilities that go beyond the traditional technology SOC and NOC, and add risk operations center (ROC) concepts. An ROC takes data from the asset risk assessments, third-party risk assessments, vulnerability management, and ticketing systems to provide a near-real-time risk view of an asset. An example of the value of a near-real-time view of an asset is that it can assist the business leader's understanding of whether their information could be compromised, when technology might need to schedule downtime, or prepare them to make the investment to upgrade or change the technology focus on how the business or business unit is operating. Think of the ROC as providing key inputs for a Six Sigma lean program.

The future of the SOC is constantly evolving to meet the demands of data, which in turn helps build decision support structures for leaders, with artificial intelligence (AI) and machine learning (ML) assisting more in identifying events or anomalies within data sets, as well as taking the human-to-machine interactions further by reducing the need for a level-1 analyst. With AI and ML continuing to enhance the organization there are some technologies today that are creating self-identifying and self-fixing technologies to support an organization's help desk. Budgets and workforces are evolving dynamically to take care of and fix technology before it becomes an operational outage.

 NOTES

- Most organizations are wasting money for basic SOC services. The basic SOC provides no value for the leader.
- Larger companies will build their own SOC, but it is a large investment and skill sets could become static due to either turnover or lack of movement, but this is not always the case.
- The foundation of an SOC is to establish a framework of technology, people, and processes to address most prevalent threats and move beyond ad hoc responses.

- Next-gen SOCs should move from a reactive approach to a proactive approach, enabling them to disrupt an attack life cycle early on.
- The defining elements of next-gen SOCs are proactive and/or have early detection, and faster response and remediation, thereby increasing the cyber resilience posture of an organization.
- Faster Detection + Faster Response = Improved Cyber Resilience.

CHAPTER SEVEN

CI-DR™ Key Capability Cyber Threat Intelligence

Many intelligence reports in war are contradictory;
even more are false, and most are uncertain.
What one can reasonably ask of an officer is that
he should possess a standard of judgment, which
he can gain only from knowledge of men and
affairs and from common sense. He should be
guided by the laws of probability. These are
difficult enough to apply when plans are drafted
in an office, far from the sphere of action; the task
becomes infinitely harder in the thick of fighting
itself, with reports streaming in.

– Carl von Clausewitz, Prussian general

T HE INTELLIGENCE and National Security Alliance's (INSA) stated that there is an urgent need for businesses and our government to develop high-level cyber intelligence as a way to combat the unacceptable levels of online security threats because the current "patch-and-pray" system won't cut it in the future.

Cyber intelligence within the CI-DR™ program is a key capability, as this is where the critical intelligence requirements (CIRs) and priority intelligence requirements (PIRs) from leadership get answered. They provide the strategies for collecting data to turn into "knowledge" from their analysis and understanding of the business and its digital operations. Like many cyber intelligence programs there are many components that fall under the umbrella of this higher level capability. There are forms of technical intelligence (TECHINT) specifically as it relates to platforms, applications, and systems that fall under cyber intelligence. As we mentioned previously this would include counterintelligence and forms of MASINT (measurement and signature intelligence) and of course pure signals intelligence within the digital operational environment where commerce is done today. Of course, cyber intelligence capability could not be complete without some OPFOR INT (opposing force intelligence). Any intelligence program cannot be effective without understanding the adversary.

As you can visually see as part of the CI-DR framework and naming convention, the first part is cyber intelligence. Without this capability a proper risk model or risk decision is absent key information. All information in the CI-DR program culminates and is analyzed in this capability, and all reporting and cybersecurity directions come from this capability. So let us begin to describe what is included in this capability. As we previously discussed, a commercial CI program follows the same procedures for analysis, with similar request structures; e.g. CIRs and PIRs coming from leadership and similar skills and disciplines are needed. INSA describes cyber intelligence as the products and processes across the intelligence cycle of assessing the capabilities, intentions, and activities – technical and otherwise – of potential adversaries and competitors in the cyber domain (with cyber counterintelligence as a subdiscipline).[1] We will continue with their definition as they consider both cyber counterintelligence and cyber threat intelligence (CTI) as subcomponents or disciplines. They also address key skills, and have five competencies, which we will begin with and expand into the CI-DR framework.

---

[1] Cyber Intelligence Taskforce, Cyber Intelligence: Preparing Today's Talent for Tomorrow's Threats, 2015 INSA.

The five competencies that INSA describes are technical, knowledge management, analytical, contextual domain, and communications and organizational:

Technical – the understanding of the hardware and software of information and communications technology, especially as they relate to cybersecurity.

Knowledge management and information science – the foundation for planning and organizing information collection (collection management), applying tools to gather and support complex data and information analysis and presentation.

Analytical – the human science basis for complex analysis of data and information from a variety of sources, including foundations of strategy, critical and systems thinking, reasoning and logic, problem-solving, and decision-making.

Contextual – the sector-specific, national, regional, and sociocultural foundations for analyzing complex problems; identifying key actors and roles; assessing perceptions, interests, and intentions; sensemaking; drawing inferences from actions and behaviors; and discerning situational influences.

Communications and organizational competencies – emphasize clear expression of opinions and reasoning, along with effective communication of one's ideas in writing, oral presentation, and visual display, as well as project management skills.[2]

As we described previously, the cyber intelligence capability is differentiated from CTI in that CTI is a subcomponent or a discipline of cyber intelligence. CTI is a subcomponent of an overall cyber intelligence capability and part of the connective tissue that is important to a CI-DR program. CTI is a specific discipline and capability for identifying and analyzing digital and electronic threats to an organization or systems and is a key capability for risk assessments. As previously mentioned in the chapter on cyber intelligence and how the intelligence life cycle's components interact, cyber threat intelligence as part of the overall cyber intelligence capabilities is also focused on analysis. The analysis is specific to assess threats to an organization or information system and analysts must be able to describe the threat and the nature of how it will impact the organization. Additionally, responsibilities of a CTI analyst would be to monitor emerging and

---

[2] Cyber Intelligence Taskforce, Cyber Intelligence: Preparing Today's Talent for Tomorrow's Threats, 2015 INSA page 7.

dormant cyber threats and to document and report on tactics, techniques, and procedures (TTPs).[3] Analysts also use these TTPs to identify the threat source and look to attribute a group, nation, industry exploit, or the next phase of an attack method an adversary may make. A CTI analyst may also provide recommendations on countermeasures to remediate a vulnerability or thwart any of the TTPs. A countermeasure can be any action, device, procedure, or technique that opposes a threat, vulnerability, or attack.[4] A countermeasure can also be simply translated into security controls or safeguards.[5]

To build and operate a CTI program, an organization can approach three distinct types. These three types can be dependent on the organization's size, resources, and budgets. The three types are outsourced, insourced, or co-sourced. An organization may choose the outsourced model to leverage their MSSP or SOC in collecting and reporting on cyber threats to the organization. As mentioned previously in connection with next-gen SOC, an organization can build all these capabilities internally, or co-source capabilities between vendors, partners, and internal staff with capabilities located in different business functions. Co-sourcing can begin to leverage cyber fusion centers and their ability to validate and contextualize information into knowledge. Analysts from other disciplines can support many of the CTI analysts and may provide a different perspective, which is important when building a "knowledge" package for leadership.

Most cyberattacks leave behind forensic evidence that can be used to assess the capabilities of the attacker. This is one of the connective tissues as to why we have the forensic capability integrated with the CI-DR program to be able to assist in discerning information. With all the attacks that have taken place, there is significant intelligence out there about techniques, cyber weapons, and strategies that have been used in these cyber assaults. Analysis of this evidence can create those TTPs which will help to identify the source of the malicious intent. The *Cyber Commander's Handbook* identifies that these TTPs create a digital DNA pertaining to an attack. Digital DNA stands for the knowledge repository that stores cyberattack analysis. ASDF represents the four digital DNA characteristic sets. Included in this repository are the following:

- A = attributes, abilities, abstraction, architecture, assembly, adaptation
- S = style, signatures, syntax, structure, source, specification, scope

---

[3] DOD, JP 1-02 *DoD Dictionary of Military and Associated Terms*, 8 November 2010 Amended 15 February 2016).

[4] Committee on National Security Systems, CNSS Instruction No. 4009, 2010, https://www.hsdl .org/?abstract&did=7447.

[5] Joint Task Force Transformation Initiative, NIST SP 800-53 revision 4, US Department of Commerce, 2013, http://dx.doi.org/10.6028/NIST.SP.800-53r4.

- D = demographics, delivery, development, discipline, data, design
- F = functions, features, faults, formidability, fields, form, factors

The digital DNA code analysis, attack vector mapping, and tracing of malicious code assist in the attribution function of cyberattack investigations. Digital DNA analysis capabilities are seen as being critical to cyber defense and cyber intelligence, as well as holding those who choose to launch cyberattacks accountable for their actions.[6]

LinkedIn is the dominant social networking site for professionals. In 2011 there were multiple instances of what are being referred to as virtual cyber spies. Multiple users reported a phishing expedition to identify and engage information operations (IO) experts and others on LinkedIn. They've reported invitations from an individual calling himself George W. who purports to be "Colonel Williams," an "IO professional" in the Washington DC area. Invitations, with a number of wording variations, have been received by a number of active duty IO personnel recently. Investigation by several others has shown that the profile is for a nonexistent person. This is clearly the evolution of espionage and you can expect to see much more of this kind of activity from now on.[7] It is valuable for commercial, not just government, organizations to be cautious of cyber and physical espionage. Due to the nature of espionage activities in the commercial sector there are no clear metrics showing the loss of a compromise to vital operational, intellectual, or other tangible assets. However, CTI can be leveraged within the digital or cyberspace to determine false campaigns, or product similarities entering the market, by using TTPs to determine if there is a threat to the organization. The forensic capabilities will be discussed in upcoming chapters.

Another aspect of CTI that can be used by a commercial organization is during a merger or acquisition. The CTI program can identify potential leakage of information, and can assist in performing a cyber due diligence looking for previous or potential compromises in the new company. This activity can save considerable money and provide a smoother transition for each company as they integrate disparate systems and processes. As we mentioned previously in Chapter 6, this capability can be insourced or outsourced, and it is valuable and beneficial to have someone internally overseeing and providing the CIRs and PIRs to this group. Additionally, the CTI program can be fully implemented and decentralized across business units to provide expertise for a particular operation or leader. This is similar to how the military would work, where each battalion commander and above would have their own intelligence shop, responsible for providing collections, analysis, dissemination,

---

[6] Kevin Colman, *Cyber Commander's Handbook*, Association for Computing Machinery, 2013 v 4.
[7] Ibid.

and decision structures for the leaders. Commercial business leaders already do this with business intelligence and big data initiatives; the external and internal cyber threat component can be integrated there, or be part of a larger fusion team.

A CTI team must also have available similar capabilities and support like the business intelligence analyst in that they collect business objectives and direction. Ingesting data from internal systems is part of the overall CI-DR program where information from training and awareness, asset risk rssessments, third-party assessments, internal audit, independent audits, vulnerability management, application and security testing, forensic investigations, eDiscovery activities, etc., all flows into the cyber intelligence capability and is evaluated and analyzed by the CTI program. External threat feeds are also extremely important to the program's maturity and overall effectiveness. External threat feeds in the past were costly and were usually provided by an external third party; this is similarly true today, but there are more companies providing that data, and many of the larger Fortune 100 companies have developed many of those in-house, and many rival the U.S. government's abilities. These external threat feeds are what happens in the darkest corners of the internet, including on normal internet, deep web, dark web, and social media sites hosted in these three areas. There is no adequate source for companies to guide them as to which service to purchase or which company can provide the best external feeds. Gartner has many listed as the best, but they may not be relevant to your industry. You will want to have your external threat feeds specific to your industry and assets.

For example, if you are a government contractor, in the manufacturing vertical you may want to focus your threat collections within the defense industrial base, industrial control systems, and geopolitical issues in your regions. Many of the geopolitical activities have directly contributed to attacks being launched or specific counteractions from cyber activities. We have seen this against sites when treaties change, or nuclear or financial summits break down; geopolitics are directly related to cyber threats. Getting the right threat package is essential to creating the right profile and decision points for your consumers.

There are many books and whitepapers on cyber threat intelligence and we are therefore not going to cover many those aspects here. This chapter is for the business leader to understand that CTI is a capability that must be leveraged to ensure current and emerging threats are part of the overall "knowledge" package being presented. CTI can be a part of the overall message and communications to executives and other governance meetings to show trending and emerging threats to the business line, company, and industry.

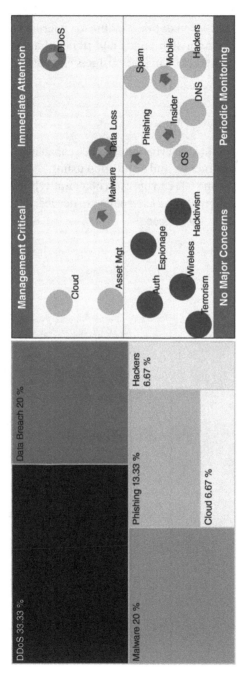

FIGURE 7.1 Threat reporting.

It validates the resources that the security team may be cycling and requesting business systems to be hardened or taken offline for upgrades, etc. Figure 7.1 provides leadership with discussion points and trends that can help identify changes or provide cautious action in how business can operate.

 NOTES

- CTI is a subcomponent of the cyber intelligence capability.
- It can be leveraged by merger and acquisition teams.
- Business intelligence and CTI can operate collaboratively in a fusion center.
- Threat feeds both internally and externally are needed; it is a value expenditure to have the right threat feeds.

CHAPTER EIGHT

CI-DR™ Key Capability Forensic Teams

Dr. Steven Johnson

P RIVATE ORGANIZATIONS struggle to identify the appropriate use for a forensic capability. Muddied by Hollywood and stigmatized for its close association with law enforcement, the utility an adequately employed forensic capability brings to an organization's ability to properly respond to incidents is understated. The application of forensic principles is at the core of properly assessed cyber threat intelligence. In fact, cyber threat intelligence is not possible without the application of human intervention and, as such, the use of forensic technique enhances the accuracy, validity, and application of cyber threat intelligence when managing risk before, during, and at the conclusion of an incident.

To first understand digital forensics it is important to establish a common lexicon; often in the realm of cyberspace and the practice of cybersecurity – words matter. The professional practice of cybersecurity is not yet standardized, as is shown with the myriad frameworks and schemas available for managing cyber risks, and because of this words may take on specific or unique meanings based upon the context in which terminology is used. This issue persists when talking about digital forensics, as there are nuances between terms when used in the context of law enforcement/litigation or private applications and incident investigations; the target audience for this text is the latter so we will focus there.

The term "forensics" is derived from the Latin words "forum" and "forensis," meaning "in open court." These two words together form the basis for "forensic" – for the courts. Regardless of your end audience your "court" may be different – either in the traditional sense of judge and jury or in a practical application sense of internal counsel, internal audit, the chief information security officer, a board of directors, regulators, and so on. Although the work of a private forensic practitioner may never see a traditional courtroom or legal proceeding, the approach and discipline required to meet the burden of scientific process should not be undercut.

In legal proceedings, artifacts entered into the case record are called evidence. Digital forensics is employed to acquire, analyze, and report on electronic evidence. Electronic evidence can be stored on physical devices such as hard drives or CDs and logical devices like network-attached storage, email servers, and public/private cloud environments. Yes, these environments are at some point in the technology stack supported by physical servers and storage arrays; however, from an investigative standpoint it may be impractical to analyze vast compute or storage environments. Digital evidence acquired and analyzed forensically is done so through the application of scientifically applied methodologies and tools. The forensic analysis of digital evidence should be rooted in fact and ambiguity should be limited at all cost. Often in the pursuit of an investigation, a forensic practitioner is limited to determining the evidence to be inconclusive. This can be frustrating, and in the realm of cyberspace, where information is volatile and anonymity is quite easy, the application of results derived from forensic analysis can be used during the assessment of cyber threat intelligence but the two should never coincide. Instead, the application of digital forensics should be the connective tissue between fact and the theoretical when assessing attribution, methods, and means of cyber threat actors.

Before we begin to discuss the forensics process, its practical applications, and how to implement a digital forensic capability within your organization, it is important to take a moment to state what digital forensics is *not*. Among other things, digital forensics is not:

- Network security
- Reverse malware engineering

- Threat hunters
- Intrusion detection specialists
- Cyber defense
- E-discovery
- Platform security
- Security event monitoring (SEIM)

It is true, digital forensics can act as a support function when achieving the mission each of these practices are designed to do. All too often, organizations fail to implement the rigor necessary to attain a level of efficacy to establish a proper forensic capability. The bar is set high. Intentionally so: any work product completed under the guise of the term "forensic" must be defensible. We'll talk about what *defensible* in the sense of digital forensics means in a moment.

The takeaway here is that organizations are full of talented technologists, some of whom are truly experts in their given field. Unless these individuals are also properly trained in the application of forensic science, you're running the risk of invalidating any findings or analysis these individuals complete. People often view digital forensic analysts as "computer experts" but the truth is that a properly trained and certified digital forensic examiner is an expert in nothing more than the digital forensic process. Yes, they might have expert-level training in another discipline (say malware reverse engineering), but as a stand-alone, they are technology generalists with expert-level knowledge of the methods used to acquire, analyze, and report on digital evidence.

Entire textbooks have been published outlining, to varying levels of specificity, the forensic process. Regardless of the forensic disciplnee all forensic processes can be generalized to the methods by which evidence is acquired, analyzed, and reported on. Digital forensics is no exception and highlighted below are the core elements of each phase as it relates to the practice. This chapter is not meant to replace formal forensic training and does not go to the level of detail necessary to satisfy all of the forensic principles but rather is a benchmark to ensure you have thought about and considered the breadth of the practice when implementing your own forensic capability.

Acquiring digital evidence begins with adequately identifying sources of potential evidence. At the onset of an investigation it may not be readily apparent the location of potential digital evidence. When employing digital forensic techniques within a corporate environment, the value of verbose system, platform, application, and network logging becomes apparent. In a law enforcement setting the challenge of identifying digital artifacts to use in the course of an investigation becomes much more difficult and it may be best to employ a "collect all" approach. Keeping in the spirit of the text to a traditional corporate environment, we'll table the law enforcement element for another time.

Acquiring digital artifacts should be considered long before an investigation is initiated and prior to an incident ever occurring. Verbose logging and monitoring considerations should be carefully examined at the stage of system implementation and throughout a systems life cycle. Technology executive management (chief information officer (CIO), chief technology officer (CTO), chief information security officer (CISO), etc.) together should establish enterprise norms and guiding principles regarding the firm's acceptable practices around system logging, monitoring, and retention.

Whether an organization elects to staff a forensic capability internally or through a third-party service provider, these experts should be consulted when developing the firm's logging and monitoring practices to ensure evidence acquisition requirements are considered. Each organization is unique and will have both unique data capture and/or retention requirements but also an appetite for the level of detail logging should reach. Depth and breadth of logging will be heavily influenced by the volume of logging from a pure size and scale perspective, the tooling in place, and the level of capture detail. Simply stated, logging everything is impractical. A decision might also need to be made regarding a trade-off between logging detail and the length of time the logging is retained.

To aid in this decision-making process, cyber threat intelligence can be employed to conduct a scenario analysis of likely attack vectors an organization might be faced with. A system's logging and monitoring approach can then be informed by the likely attack patterns or techniques. Part of this scenario analysis should also include the development of incident response procedures for the various attack types. I like to call these procedures "playbooks." All organizations have myriad policies, standards, and procedures. While a playbook might include predetermined response procedures it could also incorporate nontactical response objects like preapproved corporate communications, call tree references, regulatory reporting requirements, and other useful information. Playbooks are elevated to a higher significance than your typical "procedure." It is also important to note that creation and approval of playbooks should involve all stakeholders needed during an incident response. The same is true for an acquisition plan.

It is imperative that a forensic professional, either internal or third-party, is operating under proper authorization. Authority to conduct a forensic process should be vetted and approved both from an organizational perspective (typically through general counsel or similar) and also with the business and technical system owners. This agreement should clearly establish the rules of engagement and how a firm intends to employ digital forensics and the stated outcome. Technical owners (CIO, CTO, etc.) should be aware of the intent for a forensic examination. Internal forensic teams often have elevated or administrator entitlements across the enterprise – the approval and recertification of which potentially may be used to codify a granted authority. Firms using third-party forensic services should ensure authority and remit are clearly stated within a properly executed statement of work (SOW).

Within the confines of a corporate environment, the practical acquisition of digital evidence is relatively straightforward. Evidence gathered will likely be sourced from physical end user computing devices such as desktops and laptops – the capability to acquire evidence from mobile devices should be considered as well. For most cybersecurity investigations, network devices will provide useful information in the form of port configuration states, access control lists, or any deterministic routing configurations. The physical seizure of networking devices is often not necessary – just be prepared to have the knowledge and tooling to acquire this information. Enterprise class software and most internet-facing applications employ application-level logging. Application logging may provide a granular level of detail in order to recreate user actions that allow for a very precise timeline recreation. In addition to user data, application logs may also provide connectivity information. Internet-facing applications often record IP addresses and other connectivity information. Application logs may also be able to capture file upload/download information as well. Application form input data can prove useful in most common cybersecurity investigations, as attackers will look to exploit cross-site scripting (XSS) vulnerabilities of internet-facing applications. If an application employs any logging of unsuccessful form inputs, rejected input validations, etc., this information may give a forensic investigator a jumpstart on their analysis by examining the log files for unsuccessful exploit attempts.

The retrieval of network log files will almost always be required in some form. Absent robust application or platform (e.g. operating system) logging, network logs will enable a forensic investigator to piece together a timeline of action. Network logs often contain information relevant to system authentication and access requests; even absent application logging most organizations leverage Active Directory or some central form of identity management. If user sign-on action is absent from a system or application log file, network log files may contain user authentication information, enabling a forensic investigator to establish attribution, or ownership, of a particular action. Network log files may also establish a preliminary chain of events. A variety of systems maintain connection persistence once a user is authenticated; by examining connect and disconnect characteristics an examiner can home in on potential start and end attributes of an attack. There is one last important point relative to network logs. Network logs are a great location to answer the often-asked questions, "Did a malicious actor breach our network? What might they have access to or what might they have taken?" These are complex questions, the context of which is discussed in the chapter on incident response. Absent extremely verbose logging, often it is impossible to answer these questions definitively. Network logging, through the examination of packet captures or similar, may enable an investigator to determine what if anything might have been exfiltrated. Even for encrypted network traffic, volumetric analysis may be employed to examine actual activity versus expected known behavior of a system or application.

Platform and infrastructure logging should be considered together. The heavy use of virtualization among corporate enterprises, as well as the rapid adoption of cloud computing environments, has muddied the traditional independence of operating system and hardware. Traditional virtual compute environments employ hardware called hypervisors, which act as the "infrastructure" a runtime environment is executed up. Typically this is some sort of operating system, such as Microsoft Windows or various versions of Unix and Linux. A particular challenge when acquiring digital evidence within these environments is determining to what level of granularity a collection must be executed. Because the platform resources are virtualized it may be necessary and prudent to collect evidence at the hypervisor level. Collections at a hypervisor level may introduce privacy or compliance implications due to the one-to-many relationship of the compute environment. Put another way, when acquiring evidence at the hypervisor level you may be collecting evidence pertinent to all the virtual environments supported by that host.

Cloud computing environments are poised with similar challenges to on-premises virtual environments with additional added complexities. The primary challenge with the collection of evidence within cloud computing environments is the limited visibility and control. This, of course, is dependent on what type of cloud computing environment one is dealing with. Platform as a service presents a different set of circumstances than infrastructure as a service environments. Private cloud installations may solve some of these challenges; however, a pragmatic way to frame this concern is the "as a service" element of your target cloud computing environment, as this will commonly be where acquisition difficulties arise. An organization must realize this as a potential delimiter to the benefits a leveraged cloud computing environment brings. It is important to establish an understanding as to the level of accessibility an organization has to its cloud environment prior to evoking incident response and the need for forensic investigation. An organization must also know to what level of service or assistance a cloud provider is willing to support for incident response. This understanding should be captured in cloud computing agreements and define how an organization engages with the service provider to obtain evidences and support for its incident response needs.

State persistence may also be a concern in virtualized or cloud environments. It is common practice to redeploy operating systems or applications in these dynamic compute environments. Many benefits come from this practice, such as security and user feature release. The danger is also present when an organization is slow to detect a potential incident. This may introduce a scenario where by a system has been rebuilt prior to an organization realizing an incident has occurred, potentially destroying valuable artifacts.

In summary, the acquisition of digital evidence should be considered prior to the need to collect digital evidence. Enterprise management should carefully consider data retention and acquisition needs when establishing a robust logging and monitoring strategy. Great care should be given to balance the length of retention with the volume of data retained. It is all too often a situation where the ramifications of disparate logging practices are felt once an incident is limited in its investigation because relevant and necessary data had not been captured or retained.

The ability to conduct a comprehensive forensic analysis is limited by the ability to identify and acquire digital evidence.

Before the topic of forensic analysis can be covered we must address the forensic lab environment. When one hears the term "forensic," the image of white lab coats and sterile environments is often envisioned and these are, in fact, true necessities for some forensic analysis. The physical environment can have an impact on the outcome of a digital forensic examination. To avoid any potential bias of the examination outcome or, in the extreme, unintentional destruction of data, we need to ensure a proper lab environment is in place.

The forensic lab environment should be closed off and secured from access by any nonessential personnel. It is good practice to employ a deterministic access control mechanism (ID cards, biometric, etc.) and to keep an accurate record or log of visitors not enrolled in the lab's authentication mechanism. The principal concept of "chain of custody" is of utmost importance. Chain of custody maintains a record of the disposition and receivership of evidence. This could be digital transfer or physical. For physical evidence such as laptops or cell phones, an evidence locker should be employed. The term "locker" is used loosely – evidence could be stored in a room, closet, lockbox, safe, or any other mechanism to ensure only those intended to access the evidence are able to. For evidence stored digitally it is good practice to have storage devices that are gapped from the corporate network and have host-based access control mechanisms. Two-factor authentication is a nice-to-have as well.

The physical lab environment should be adequately temperature controlled. With significant disk storage sizes commonly found today, a terabyte or more will require overnight imaging or indexing – coming back to the office the next day to find the temperature in the lab to be excessive and hardware failure as a result is an unpleasant experience. Also take care to avoid water. It seems simple but is often overlooked. Work with your organization's facilities professionals to locate space for a lab out from under a potential leaky toilet or HVAC pipe which might condensate; these are realistic scenarios that potentially may compromise your lab environment. It is also pragmatic to avoid carpeted spaces; office furniture with anti-static desktop properties is widely available within the marketplace. Anti-static mats and wristlets are also an option.

For forensic practitioners operating in a corporate environment it is my recommendation to air-gap your lab, both physically and wirelessly. Network and other enterprise administrators traditionally have elevated privileges – to avoid potential compromise, establishing an analysis environment separate from a broader corporate network will ensure you do not have to, with each investigation, address this point of concern. It's also good practice, given forensics is usually reserved for sensitive investigations. The simplest way to implement this strategy, given most forensic persons work entirely within the lab environment, is to have dedicated workstations for forensic analysis, and workstations for access to corporate resources (email, intranet, etc.).

Aside from maintaining a strict chain of custody and preserving the sensitivity of an investigation, forensic analysis can be dangerous. Although not physically harmful, it is common practice to detonate malware samples and other malicious code in due course of a forensic investigation. Reverse malware engineering and malware analysis are routinely invoked in support of incident response within enterprise compute environments. Air-gapping the forensic lab and analysis machine is a pragmatic solution to a very real scenario of malware being inadvertently exposed to the corporate network. Air-gapping the forensic lab (you may even want to consider limiting the connectivity between forensic workstations within the lab) helps reduce the risk of malware exposure.

This isn't a how-to on forensic analysis but here's a pro tip – many of you are likely reading this and thinking, "Doesn't a lot of malware know when it's not connected to the internet and hibernate?" Sure, a lot of malware does. One of the principal traits of a digital forensic examiner is ingenuity. Whether in the field or back at the lab, the use of cellular hotspot devices (such as a MiFi) can be used to provide a channel for detonated malware to sense an internet connection and reach out to a command-and-control server.

Once the lab environment has been established, we can turn our attention to executing the forensic analysis. Great care must be taken to avoid completing analysis on the original evidence. To clarify: a log file dumped from a system is the original evidence, not the resident log file itself. This is a clear distinction to make; all too often I have seen a log file procured, worked with, and then compromised in some way, only to then be unable to re-collect the evidence. This could be due to the clearing of a log file, log dropoff, or that someone simply rebuilt a machine because they thought "the forensic person has it." The same point can be made with system-level acquisitions as well.

It may be impractical to physically acquire the evidence and therefore the system must be collected through other mechanisms. Say, for example, you are a forensic examiner working for a global organization. You might be tasked with conducting analysis on a system halfway around the globe and elect to complete a bitwise disc image across the network. This takes time and you might only have one shot at doing so. If you begin analyzing the disc image and it is destroyed or compromised, again you might have missed your shot.

Although one could argue your disc image or log file is just a "copy," make a copy of your copy and treat the initial copy as though you were in possession of a physical original. When working with physical originals there are some tools you need to ensure are in the toolbox. For working with physical hard discs or memory stick (e.g. thumb drive) the use of a write blocker is required. A write blocker prevents the disc from being written to inadvertently. Some discs, when mounted, may alter the disc's boot record or other data elements on the drive.

The forensic copy is a like-for-like replica of the original artifact. In terms of forensic analysis, practitioners use the terminology "imaging" when referring to the process by which a forensic copy is made. When replicating hard drives or other physical devices a bitwise copy is the preferred method to replicate data. A bitwise copy captures and allocates an unallocated addressable drive space, which enables an investigator to leverage data-carving techniques to retrieve previously deleted files or partially overwritten files. Absent the ability to obtain a bitwise copy, logical replicas can be made.

Logical images will be commonplace in corporate environments where it is impractical to seize or have access to physical underlying hardware to collect a bitwise image from. Examples of proper use cases to leverage logical imaging include network file shares, system logs, mainframe environments, and cloud or remotely located compute environments. The logical imaging process varies based on the tooling employed when securing a logical image; however, most of these tools will place a logical file into some type of digital container to limit the potential for alteration once the files are collected.

During the imaging process, be it logical or physical, most tools will also perform a hash value calculation on the image file, enabling the forensic investigator to attain a digital signature of the image. Saving the detailed explanation of how a hash value is derived, the key concept to learn here is what a hash value is used for in the context of digital forensics. A hash value is derived through the use of a mathematical algorithm to produce a hash value. Common hashing algorithms are MD5, SHA1, SHA256, and for the purpose of attaining a digital signature, any of these algorithms can be used.

Hashing is used as a form of digital signature because, like human DNA, no two hash profiles are the same. If one bit of a file or file system being hashed is changed, the resulting output from the hashing process will change as well. In full disclosure there have, in very controlled environments, been instances wherein a hash collision has been produced. A collision occurs when two disparate files produce the same hash output. This scenario is caused by limitations in certain hash algorithms in extreme long-tail experiments; this bears little implication to practical application of hash methodology in an examination. It is more important for an investigator to be aware of the potentiality than to employ overburdened (i.e. longer to process) hashing algorithms. Pragmatically, sticking to the use of MD5 or SHA256 will avoid most of this uncertainty.

A quick mention on mobile devices. Firstly, these devices can be quite volatile, meaning changes to a power state (either through power off or battery depletion) may destroy artifacts potentially useful to an investigation. Second, connectivity either through Wi-Fi or cellular networks reduces the confidence of an investigator to state proper chain of custody as discussed above, since the devices can be interacted with remotely. Third, hardware-level encryption on many of these devices makes it particularly difficult to gain access to from an analysis perspective.

To protect mobile devices for transport and analysis it is critical the device is placed into a faraday bag. A faraday bag is lined with a protective layer, which blocks the reception or transmission of wireless signals to the device. Many faraday bags are clear or transparent, enabling an investigator to see the device while it is protected. Some faraday bag manufacturers have models which can accommodate touchscreen interaction through the protective layers of the bag or have the ability to keep a device charged while in the bag so as to not lose potential data or alter the state of the device once seized. If you are working in a corporate environment, it may be beneficial to have the user unlock the device and then either change the pass lock or prevent the device from auto-locking, as having operating system–level access to the device may provide you with better options for analysis. Still, depending on the device, an investigator's only option may be a manual scroll or viewing of the content stored on the device.

Related to mobile devices but generally important for those working in corporate environments is privacy. While forensics is most often associated with law enforcement investigations, the uses of forensic techniques within the private sector are valid. A variable introduced is from the perspective of individual privacy. For corporate-owned assets, data, and compute environments, most firms employ an acceptable use policy which will dictate the remit of individual monitoring and right to investigate. With the increasing adoption of bring your own device (BYOD) policies, the accessibility of and the ability to acquire and analyze potential targets may be limited. A common scenario encountered is corporate data or artifacts residing on a device owned by an individual – always consult with legal counsel prior to the attempted acquisition of BYOD-type device, and certainly always personal devices not subject to BYOD governance. The lack of clear authorization in any forensic investigation immediately calls into jeopardy the integrity of the overall process.

Moving beyond the nuances when preparing digital evidence for analysis, the software toolkit used is parallel to the scientific tools used in other forensic disciplines. Like a sterile and well-maintained physical lab environment, the digital lab environment must be treated with care. It is good practice to record the details of the physical hardware being used. Examples of this include hardware manufacturer (if not built and assembled by you), the make, model, and serial numbers for the CPU, motherboard, storage devices, memory, peripheral devices, and power supplies. This is to ensure that, if required, an independent investigator could replicate the exact conditions under which digital evidence was analyzed. Additionally, if for some reason in the future a defect in the manufacturing of a device proves to have compromised the investigation, you will need the ability to understand the implication to past casework. My preference is to keep every analysis with a case log, or noted record, and place these details as a compendium to my analysis notes.

As with hardware, so should software be documented in sufficient detail to enable an independent investigator to replicate the environment under which a forensic examination was conducted. Documentation of software components used should include firmware and BIOS makes and versions, operating system versions, including what level of patching has been applied, commercial off-the-shelf products, including version numbers and license or access codes. There are fantastic open-sourced forensic toolkits; the nature of open-sourced software means modification and distribution may be suspect. When using open-sourced software be sure to document the acquisition method and location and preserve a copy of the software binaries in the event you need to provide these to an independent investigator as well.

Regardless of the tools used during an investigation, the importance of tool validation cannot be understated. As with many scientific instruments, there is a need for maintenance calibration, and training is required before these tools can be used. In the case of digital forensics it is critical that the forensic practitioner is properly trained in the use of the chosen toolset and can demonstrate proficiency if need be. There is a vast vendor marketplace for digital forensic tools – both physical (write blockers, mobile acquisition tools, etc.) and digital (analysis suites and bespoke purpose tools). The benefit of the support in the marketplace by vendors is many will offer training programs, certification testing, or both. My general advice would be, if you are using a tool and a training program or certification in the use of the tool is available – complete it. It's much easier to produce a training record or certificate demonstrating competency in a tool than having to demonstrate or explain it away.

One final note on software and software-based tools: ensure that you have proper licensing to use the software for your purpose. This could be as simple as ensuring your organization has licensed the operating system you are using to more complex situations, such as using open-sourced software for commercial gains. Again, nothing will discredit the findings of an investigation more than discrediting the integrity of the investigator or the investigative process.

At this point in the analysis process your digital lab environment is equipped with the tools needed to conduct a comprehensive examination. Take the time now to validate your tooling using practice or "dummy" cases. A fun exercise is to hop online to your favorite bidding site and buy an old, cheap laptop and have fun! By purchasing something a bit old and less mainstream you can put to test your ability to handle anything strange or uncanny when in the field. Acquiring something of the unknown will also enable you to put to the test your sleuthing abilities to take a piece of "evidence" and see what can be seen when you don't have much by means of clues to work from. This will also ensure all of your tools are working in harmony and functioning as expected before you are tasked with analyzing "real" evidence.

The software tools in the forensic toolkit are the sole choice of the investigator and I will not persuade you with my personal preferences. In reality, it's best to have a variety of tools, as I have found there is no one forensic suite that will meet all needs. Tool selection will depend heavily on the nature of the evidence needing to be analyzed. For example, there are specialist tools for Macintosh operating systems, others more suited for Windows or Linux-based systems, and even tools designed specifically for mobile devices. Being equipped with a variety of tools will ensure you can approach most any investigation encountered in the field.

Forensic investigators working in a corporate environment may be able to select specific tooling to suit the compute environments of the work. For example, many intrusion detection systems (IDS) have analysis "sandboxes" and other proprietary software which can aid an investigation. Forensic professionals in a corporate environment will frequently be called upon during the investigation of malware infections – the application of traditionalist forensic tooling may be too slow or too cumbersome to answer basic attribution or function analysis of malware. I will leave it to you for the precise selection of tools and leave you with a few summary points.

In summary, the process by which a forensic examiner approaches forensic analysis is strictly influenced by the toolset chosen and the task at hand. Dedicated training courses and books have been published around topics such as mobile device forensics, network forensics, malware analysis, and others. As this text is not a strict instructional, anyone looking to implement a forensic capability within their cybersecurity program should be aware of the fundamentals. Care should be taken to properly establish a working environment supportive of forensic principles and in a way that supports chain of custody. The forensic lab environment is a specialist environment and should be treated and managed separately from a primary corporate network. Proper training must be in place; attempting to re-task network administrators or other "tech guys" to complete forensic analysis during an investigation is a short-sighted approach. The term "forensic" brings with it the responsibility to have properly trained and authorized individuals completing the task at hand; if they are not the foremost technical experts in the area of examination, have someone who is act in an advisory capacity.

All tools used should be properly licensed, installed, and validated. Detailed records of the hardware and software components used should be retained and updated so as to enable another forensic investigator to replicate the scenario under which the initial analysis first took place. Finally, all forensic activities should be vetted and authorized by organizational management, both in the establishment of the capability and in clear granted authority and clear statements as to where that authority ends. The privacy of company employees and individuals must be balanced when acquiring digital artifacts and completing analysis; if during the course of an investigation user privacy becomes a concern, pause the investigation and seek advice and reauthorization to continue.

And finally, the use of digital forensics in a corporate environment is vast but in this scenario a forensic examiner is not playing the role of law enforcement. A properly trained and licensed forensic professional will know the legal limits and implications of conducting forensic examinations in a private setting. Some jurisdictions require individuals conducting digital forensic examinations to be licensed as private investigators (PIs). And if during the course of an investigation you suspect illicit or illegal activity may be present – seek legal counsel.

How forensic examiners report their findings is a matter of preference and the purpose the forensic report serves. In legal proceedings, there exists precedent and established expectations as to the elements that should be contained within an expert witness report. Within a corporate setting, the presentation of analysis results could be via email or executive summary briefs.

When a forensics capability is paired with a capable cyber threat intelligence team, a full detailed malware analysis may be needed to derive protective countermeasures, identify additional compromised hosts, or to simply learn the tactics, techniques, and procedures (TTPs) of the threat actor. Regardless of the intent of the forensic investigation, the forensic report should be tailored to fit the needs of the consumer and should be done in a way that maintains the integrity of the findings.

At minimum, the forensic report should include relevant details so as to reconstruct a proper timeline. A forensic timeline should include both a timeline of events of the incident in question (e.g. time of exploit, time of infection, time of exfiltration) and the analysis timeline (e.g. time the evidence was seized and the sequence of analysis). Having timeline details clear and apparent will help answer a majority of the questions executive management will ask.

Perhaps not for an executive summary or tactical intelligence report, the forensic analyst should keep a detailed and secured case log. The case log should be used to capture key investigative processes, techniques used throughout the forensic analysis in sufficient detail where an independent forensic investigator could replicate your analysis and reach the same investigative outcome. In a corporate setting, most executives will not be interested in the detailed analysis log, but as a cautionary tale – do not skip this key step. Many times, following the production of an analysis I have been challenged on elements of the findings and have been asked to demonstrate how I derived these conclusions. Having the case log enables me to competently replay the analysis. Additionally, you may encounter a scenario where you (or the firm) has reached its limit on time, money, and skill set during the course of an investigation and the decision is made to engage an outside third party. Having a properly documented case log will enable you to effectively transition your casework. Also, corporate environments tend to see the same attacks and attack vectors exploited on a routine basis; having an accessible case log of historical analysis will enable you as the forensic examiner to quickly access your notes and complete an analysis following an already proven methodology. Your expedience and quick turnaround time will make you shine with the Security Incident ResponseTeam (SIRT)!

 NOTES

- Even in a rote corporate environment there lies the potential that your forensic analysis may play a role in legal proceedings. As was stated at the beginning of this chapter, what makes a forensic professional a forensicator is not their subject matter expertise in all aspects of technology. A properly trained and licensed forensic examiner is an expert in the forensic process. Their work, while supporting executive management and aiding to protect corporate environments, may be called upon for the courts.
- Acquiring digital artifacts should be considered long before an investigation is initiated and prior to an incident ever occurring.
- The forensic lab environment should be closed off and secured from access to any nonessential personnel. Additionally, the lab should be "air-gapped" from the corporate networks.
- In summary, the process by which a forensic examiner approaches forensic analysis is strictly influenced by the toolset chosen and the task at hand.
- Forensics capabilities paired with a cyber threat intelligence team can effectively provide analysis to derive protective countermeasures, and identify and learn the tactics, techniques, and procedures (TTPs) of the threat actor.
- Build your Security or Cyber Incident Response Team with certified forensic analysts.
- Integrate your forensic capabilities as shown in the CI-DR™ model.

CHAPTER NINE

CI-DR™ Key Capability
Vulnerability Management Teams

By Derek Olson

*Securing a computer system has traditionally
been a battle of wits: the penetrator tries to find
the holes, and the designer tries to close them.*

– M. Gasser

A VULNERABILITY MANAGEMENT (VM) program is a process for identifying, analyzing, and managing vulnerabilities in the technical and nontechnical environment in an organization. It affords the ability to reduce risk in the organization through a programmatic application of time, money, and resources to achieve a reduction to the threat vectors of an organization. Vulnerability management has multiple components that when working in concert becomes an instrument for connecting a Cyber Intelligence-Driven Risk (CI-DR™) program.

As with all capabilities highlighted in this book, vulnerability management is not solved by just implementing a technical scanning solution, patching vulnerabilities, and repeating the process. It requires connectivity to multiple capabilities within a CI-DR. The "connective tissue" we talk about in this book is not unidirectional but multidirectional and ties capabilities together in support of the greater program.

A VM program is intrinsically connected to both the primary and secondary objectives of a CI-DR program. In support of the primary objective a VMP facilitates all four key components. First, a VM program allows an organization to evaluate the existing conditions of an organization through the mapping of assets and exposure to threats. In support of the second component, it aids in the ability to understand the potential movement and targets of adversaries. A VM program is essentially the foundation of the third task; by design it identifies the vulnerabilities that could be exploited by an adversary. Finally, it factors into the documented knowledge that assists in the critical risk-based decision making and ultimately the course of action for an organization.

As the components of a CI-DR are not mutually exclusive, a programmatic management of vulnerabilities ties knowledge to execution in support of the second objective. Intelligence-driven decisions are based upon input from all areas of cyber risk discussed in this book. A VMP critically ties vulnerability exposure to knowledge of adversarial tactics to execution of identification and protection of an organization's assets.

To build an effective VM program in support of a CI-DR, organizations need to focus on four key components. The four components within a vulnerability management program are vulnerability identification, vulnerability analysis, vulnerability management, and the vulnerability management team.

Vulnerability identification starts with the choosing of an appropriate technological solution to support the program. There are many great solutions on the market. As this book is discussing a programmatic approach, we will not delve too far into how to choose an appropriate solution for an organization's needs. As with all technological buying decisions, organizations should understand the needs of the organization by identifying all stakeholders that may consume the output, the technology in use in an organization (some solutions may not cover all of an organization's technology), the maturity of the organization's technical and security capabilities, the technological capabilities of the solution required, and finally, budget.

When discussing "connective tissue" and its relationship to vulnerability identification, we must understand the capabilities that feed vulnerability identification and how the output nurtures other capabilities. To successfully implement a vulnerability identification, organizations need to recognize where to start the assessment, which starts with the asset management. An asset management capability traditionally provides the knowledge of what and where, ownership of the technological assets of the organization, and the criticality of those assets.

Asset management not only supports the asset risk assessment capability; its contents are also a product of the same. In order to allow for a VMP to successfully reduce risk it is critical that the information provided by an asset management capability in conjunction with the asset risk assessment capability be thorough and up to date. The input provided supplies a VM program and affords the program the data of how and where to start the assessments.

The endeavor of vulnerability identification can be a bit daunting, depending on the size and breadth of the technological footprint of an organization. The good news is that with the guidance of the asset management capability, the VM program team can start with a prioritization of discovery, including but not limited to the following guidance.

- Asset Criticality
  Critical assets are identified through the asset risk assessment process. Critical assets are typically those assets that pose an exceptional risk to the organization through application of the traditional triad of security: confidentiality, integrity, and availability (CIA). If the assets included in this are deficient in any of the CIA, there is a higher risk of loss of information, loss of revenue, or loss of reputation, to name a few.
- Asset Exposure
  The determination of where an assets lives is the second consideration. In conjunction with asset risk as described above, prioritization and cadence should be based upon the exposure of the asset.
  - Critical External Exposed Assets
    - Externally exposed critical assets if compromised pose a higher probability of an outage or disclosure of information.
  - Internal Critical Assets
    - Internal critical assets typically house the organization's "crown jewels" or are essential to ongoing business processes. If these

assets are compromised, an organization can face the loss of key data or the disruption of business, causing loss of revenue.

- Standard Assets
  - Standard assets are those assets that don't fit the preceding groups. These assets tend to include laptops, desktops, printers, etc. We talk about standard assets at a high level; this is not meant to discount the importance of these assets to an organization. It is meant to be a broad discussion. The grouping of assets can have many factors beyond criticality; it is best for each VMP team to work with asset stakeholders to best determine how to accomplish this.
- Compliance Requirements
  - Compliance can play a significant role in the requirements for vulnerability discovery. PCI, HIPAA, GLBA, and SOX are a few of the industry and regulatory frameworks requiring vulnerability identification. The VMP program should have a clear understanding of the compliance requirements that an organization is either required to or voluntarily chooses to follow, such as NIST CSF or the ISO 27000 series. With this knowledge, the VMP can determine the requirements for scope and cadence of assets included in compliance requirements.

Before a strategy for vulnerability identification can be finalized, the VMP team needs to the understand logistical categories of assets as they relate to the technologies used for identification. Regardless of the solution chosen, the scanning strategies typically include the following categories for how the identification is achieved and present factors in the VMP strategy.

- External or Remote

Assets in this scanning are typically assessed without authentication. From an external viewpoint, this scanning profile can provide an organization with an adversarial view of their vulnerability exposure. From an internal viewpoint, an unauthenticated view can provide vulnerability exposure from a rogue employee or an unauthenticated adversary in an internal environment.

- Internal or Local

Assets in this scanning profile are typically assessed with authentication and go wider and deeper than unauthenticated scanning, and includes additional checks such as configurations, software versions, and registry checks, to name just a few. This scanning profile is characteristically conducted on internally exposed assets and can provide understanding of vulnerability exposure to malicious insiders, and potential lateral movement and escalation of privileges if an adversary gained access.

■ Authenticated Agent-Based
This scanning profile, as the name suggests, uses agents on assets to perform authenticated scanning. The running agents utilize elevated privileges to identify vulnerability, like the internal scanning profile with an additional benefit, and that is that scanning can be done on offline assets, such as laptops. This factor allows those assets that are typically transitory to be scanned and then report back upon the reconnection to the management function of the scanning solution.

As a result of all of the inputs described above the VM program team is now in a position to develop a strategy for vulnerability identification to include:

■ Asset Grouping
Dependent on organization structure, asset grouping can be as simple as based upon the considerations above or can become very complex, such as with the inclusion of the aforementioned items coupled with asset stakeholders, reporting requirements, cadence needs, and maturity of an organization, to name a few.

■ Scanning Profile
Most vulnerability assessment technologies on the market utilize profiles for scanning. These profiles are typically tailored to specific platforms such as operating systems. These profiles limit the checks performed on an asset to those that are most relevant. The use of these profiles can significantly reduce scanning time as opposed to checking for everything regardless of applicability.

■ Cadence
There are many resources available to security practitioners in regard to cadence of assessments performed in the identification of vulnerabilities. Each VM program team should take multiple factors into its strategy, including but not limited to all of the aforementioned considerations such as compliance and risk, criticality combined with guidance from other capabilities such as standards and architecture, infrastructure security operations, secure coding and development, digital continuity of operations, coordination and intelligence, cyber and behavioral analytics, IT operations, and other stakeholders.

- Ad Hoc vs. Scheduled

  Typically, organizations develop a schedule for assessments based upon their strategy. However, it is a necessity to understand ad-hoc scanning and include it into its strategy. An ad-hoc scanning procedure should be developed to address significant changes to assets or environments, as well as to those needs in pre-production environments. Dependent on many of the same factors that have been previously discussed, this can typically be easy to implement, or complex due to potential technological or even license issues. An example of a license issue is that most assessment solutions are based upon IPs scanned and it is difficult to move these after the IP has been identified. This can make pre-production scans an issue, as the utilization of a license for scanning an asset, which ultimately will move to production on another IP, would consume a license. A good strategy preventing this is to allocate a license or licenses to a static set of IPs, set a schedule, such as daily, and provide the IT team those IPs. When IT teams require scanning, they move the assets to the IP to scan overnight and then remove them from that IP.

- Change Management Requirements

  Change management is the last consideration in the development of the VMP identification strategy. The change management capability is designed to understand those things that may cause adverse effects to production, understand dependencies, prevent adverse actions, and recover from any changes that cause adverse effects to the organization. Vulnerability identification through assessment can, by its technical nature, cause adverse effects to assets, especially assets that would typically fall into a legacy category. The final strategy needs processes to include the change management capability for both scheduled and ad-hoc scanning.

- Vulnerability Analysis

  With the implementation of the vulnerability identification strategy, the next step analyzing the yield of the assessments. Vulnerability analysis is an iterated process that when defined in a VMP requires a foundational organizational baseline that is articulated in the governance domain which includes the strategy and operating model and policies and standards capabilities. To aid in the analysis and management processes, the VMP team requires an organization to have documented and approved:
  - Risk appetite
  - Risk mitigation practices and policies
  - Residual risk treatment
  - Countermeasures
  - Business impact analysis

Through the clearly defined groundwork of the governance domain, The VMP team can define a strategy for analysis of discovered vulnerabilities. A vulnerability analysis strategy includes stages that are the underpinnings of the next stage of vulnerability management.

The vulnerability analysis stages are meant not only to provide the groundwork for analysis but also to fulfill compliance requirements and are considered best practices under frameworks such as NIST Special Publication 800-53 (Rev. 4), the NIST Cyber Security Framework, ISO 27001:2013, Center for Internet Security, and COBIT 5.

▪ Log Vulnerabilities

A vulnerability database is a vital resource for vulnerability assessment. It should be considered the source of truth for vulnerability management, which will be discussed in more detail in the next component section of the VMP. Depending on organizational maturity, the need for logging of vulnerability ranges from simple to complex. Contingent on the scanning technology(s) chosen, the platform(s) should provide a foundational repository for logging of vulnerabilities, allowing an organization to document its vulnerability landscape.

▪ Classification and Prioritization

Classification and prioritization are based on many organizational factors. As with much of the entire process, a documented structure always provides the best clarity for success. Basing an organizational vulnerability classification on a known standard affords an organization the ability to utilize an industry-based measurement. There are quite a few standards that are used in the industry to classify and risk-rate vulnerabilities. Choosing to apply one or a combination of these repositories will aid in the prioritization of remediation. Some of the most used guides are:

▪ Common Vulnerabilities and Exposures (CVE)
A list of common identifiers for publicly known cybersecurity vulnerabilities.[1]

▪ Common Vulnerability Scoring System (CVSS)
The Common Vulnerability Scoring System (CVSS) provides a way to capture the principal characteristics of a vulnerability and produce a numerical score reflecting its severity. The numerical score can then be translated into a qualitative representation (such as low, medium, high, and critical) to help organizations properly assess and prioritize their vulnerability management processes.[2]

---

[1] Mitre, Common Vulnerabilities and Exposures, 2020, https://cve.mitre.org/.
[2] National Institute of Technology and Standards, Common Vulnerability Scoring System v3, https://nvd.nist.gov/vuln-metrics/cvss/v3-calculator.

- Common Weakness Enumeration (CWE)
  CWE is a community-developed formal list of common software weaknesses. It serves as a common language for describing software security weaknesses, a standard measuring stick for software security tools targeting these vulnerabilities, and a baseline standard for weakness identification, mitigation, and prevention efforts.[3]
- Open Web Application Security Project (OWASP)
  The Open Web Application Security Project (OWASP) is an online community that produces freely available articles, methodologies, documentation, tools, and technologies in the field of web application security.[4]

  With the knowledge and guidance of the aforementioned vulnerability frameworks, VMP teams have the groundwork to prioritize identified vulnerabilities. The prioritization of vulnerabilities is a process of determining the relevance, compensating controls, categorization, and responsibility.

- Relevance
  When determining relevance, an organization is reliant upon other capabilities, including asset management, asset risk assessment, and the entire capability set in the assurance domain: standards and architecture, application security, secure coding and development, data risk assessment, and data loss prevention oversight.

  As described by Carnegie Mellon's CRR Supplemental Resource Guide on Vulnerability Management, "Is the vulnerability pertinent to the organization's operations? Information channels, penetration testing teams (internal and third party), and vulnerability discovery tools will produce a wealth of information. Those findings that affect only the assets the organization does not employ can be ignored, but they should be maintained for reference when planning changes to the organization. If a technology has a high vulnerability rate, the organization may decide to choose a different technology to avoid the remediation workload and associated costs."[5]

---

[3] MITRE, Common Weakness Enumeration, 2020, https://cwe.mitre.org/about/index.html.
[4] Various authors, contributors, researchers, Open Web Application Security Project, 2020, https://www.owasp.org.
[5] Carnegie Mellon University. "CRR Supplemental Resource Guide Volume 4 Vulnerability Management Version 1.1." Carnegie Melon. Accessed January 1, 2020. https://www.us-cert.gov/sites/default/files/c3vp/crr_resources_guides/CRR_Resource_Guide-VM.pdf.

- Compensating Controls
  To aid in prioritization, compensating controls (mitigation) need to be understood by the VMP team. Whether the controls are operational, preventive, or detective, established controls may in some cases reduce the risk of vulnerability exposure and in the event of no controls may raise the risk to exploitation. Understanding these controls is provided through knowledge sharing with other capabilities like that of Audit and Compliance, Infrastructure Security and Standards, and Architecture.

- Categorization
  Vulnerabilities can be categorized utilizing one of the vulnerability frameworks previously discussed. At a high level the categorization is based upon the nature of the vulnerability as determined by flaw that the vulnerability exposes. An example of some the flaws includes denial of service (DoS), code execution, overflow, memory corruption, SQL injection, XSS, directory traversal, HTTP response splitting, bypassing something, gain information, gain privileges, cross-site request forgery (CSRF), and file inclusion.[6]

- Responsibility
  The last stage is determination of responsibility. Determinant on the organization structure, determining responsibility for the vulnerability may be a single department or team or in the case of larger organizations may be broken into multiple departments, teams, or stakeholders An example of a responsibility matrix of larger organizations would be OS-based (Windows, Linux), server, database, applications, web applications, etc.

- Risk Rating
  With all of the information gathered in the previous stages, the VMP team can now apply a risk rating to the identified vulnerabilities. Most, if not all, the technologies on the market utilize a risk rating system such as CVSS to provide out-of-the-box scoring. Employing the vulnerability logging preference of the organization, the VMP team has the ability to adjust if necessary (based upon the analysis stages) the risk rating to afford the organization a better understanding of the vulnerability risk to the organization.

---

[6] Robert Auger, Web Application Consortium Threat Classification, 2012, http://projects .webappsec.org/w/page/13246978/Threat%20Classification.

- Vulnerability Management
VM can be a daunting task and prioritization can provide the means of a starting point; however, it is the beginning of the process. Dependent on the organizational risk appetite, risk mitigation strategy, and complexity of the environment, an organization's plan can be determined.
- Numbers vs. Risk
Organizational management at all levels views vulnerabilities through perspective lenses. Those lenses are determined on an individual basis. VMP teams, when working toward a vulnerability management process, need to try and understand the lens that those stakeholders are looking through.

Typically, those lenses fall into two categories: the number of vulnerabilities and the risk to the organization.

This distinction is brought up based upon professional experience. An example of this was an engagement with a large client that was engaged for vulnerability management. This client was scanning over 300,00 endpoints a month. The sheer number of vulnerabilities discovered in that monthly cadence was surprising. The organizational structure had many different departments and ultimately stakeholders to the reports produced. Management of the vulnerabilities became complex as each of the stakeholders viewed the results in the aforementioned lenses. Some were stuck on the sheer number while others understood the risk. Success by each was defined on either reduction of number of vulnerabilities or the reduction of risk.

Regardless of the lens that a stakeholder utilizes, the goal of the VMP team should be to turn a numbers conversation to risk, translating the vulnerability risk to organization risk. Taking a stakeholder's motivation, the VM program team takes the opportunity to guide the stakeholder through the process of vulnerability analysis and develop a straightforward plan to achieve a reduction of numbers, thereby reducing risk.

- Vulnerability Reporting
Whether just starting or working at a higher maturity, VM should be built on a structure that ensures that the recipient stakeholders get the information they need to help develop management plans for remediation.

Vulnerability reporting is the output of the previous components of a VM program. Reporting serves multiple purposes and is consumed by not only the stakeholders of the vulnerabilities, but also multiple capabilities under a CI-DR. As a product, reporting needs to be distributed to the appropriate responsible parties of the vulnerabilities discovered, prioritized, and risk rated. Additionally, as all five domains have connectivity to the

VMP, reporting should be shared with all of the relevant capabilities under each. For example, reporting shared with security operations for the ability to tune SOC/SIEM signatures to better prevent and detect threats, or with Intelligence and Response to understand and predict future attacks by adversaries.

Organizational report templates once agreed upon provide the VMP team the ability to consistently discuss the output regardless of recipient, thereby allowing the team to efficiently produce reports in the cadence chosen.

- Patch Management
  The NIST Special Publication 800-40 R3: Guide to Enterprise Patch Management Technologies defines patch management as "the process for identifying, acquiring, installing, and verifying patches for products and systems."[7] While patches are deployed to fix vulnerabilities in software, they may also be used for enhancements and feature changes. A patch management program when planned and executed can reduce the risk to exposed vulnerabilities as well as provide the minimum disruption to productivity.

  While the focus of this chapter is vulnerability management, patch management and vulnerability management are intrinsically tied, and they are also mutually exclusive. Not all the risks identified during vulnerability assessments require patches for remediation and not all patches are security or risk based. It is of importance to know the difference between the two processes, but also how they work in symbiosis in the pursuit of risk reduction. Using a framework like the NIST 800-40 publication mentioned above, an organization can structure an appropriate patch management program using technology and processes regardless of their current state of maturity.

  As previously discussed, the organization establishes risk tolerance and risk treatment guidelines which are incorporated in the organization's security policies and standards under the governance domain and provide a foundation for the development of path cadence and remediation scanning.

  - Cadence
    The organization's VM policy and subsequent standards are directives for developing a patch management cadence as it relates to risk.

---

[7] Murugiah Souppaya Karen Scarfone, NIST SP 800-40 revision 3, US Department of Commerce, 2013, http://dx.doi.org/10.6028/NIST.SP.800-40r3. https://nvlpubs.nist.gov/nistpubs/SpecialPublications/NIST.SP.800-40r3.pdf.

Whether on the lower maturity or at the highest level, patch management driven by the vulnerability analysis ensures the risk reduction in accordance with the organization's risk tolerance. An example of a patch management cadence based upon risk is as follows:

- Patches for critical and high-risk rated vulnerabilities must be implemented within 15 days.
- Noncritical applicable patches must be implemented within 45 days.
- System patches will be applied to all servers within 60 days of the patch release.
- Emergency (out of band) patches will be applied to all servers as soon as possible, but no later than one week after patch release.
- Vendor-supplied patch documentation will be reviewed for any major issues in order to assure compatibility with all systems components prior to being applied.
- Patches should be reviewed, evaluated, and appropriately applied after testing.
- An authorized maintenance window must be approved prior to patching systems where patches might possibly interrupt critical systems.
- In the event that a patch will not be applied due to incompatibility or risk assumption, documentation will be logged, noting the reason for not patching, and identifying additional controls to reduce risk.
- Rescan

The VM team's interaction with the patch management capability does not end with prioritization; it is in fact cyclical in nature. Upon the patch application process, the need for rescanning of assets is compulsory to assure that the vulnerability has been remediated. Dependent on the organization's change management and production requirements the rescan can occur on the next scan window, or based upon the criticality, an immediate rescan can be requested.

- Vulnerability Repository

As mentioned, the logging of vulnerabilities into a central repository is the source of truth for the vulnerability landscape of an organization. The vulnerability repository not only drives connectivity to other capabilities but as the source of truth it is also the barometer for the organization's vulnerability landscape. The repository is a living thing and changes as new vulnerabilities are identified and previously identified vulnerabilities are remediated. The chosen repository will also drive the metrics of the VMP.

- Metrics
  Metrics not only drive progress, but they can be analyzed for proper risk-based decisions. Developing a metrics component to the organization's reporting structure can be a lengthy and sometimes passionate discussion in the cybersecurity field. There are many frameworks, and some great books, like *Measuring and Managing Information Risk: A FAIR Approach* by Jack Freund and Jack Jones, which are very good sources of information for developing a program.[8]

  When discussing metrics in the VM program there are a few areas of focus that can drive maturity through the life cycle of the vulnerability management process while providing data to other connected capabilities as well as driving executive discussions.
  - Baseline
    Establishment a baseline of normal behavior is important before developing a full metrics program. This metric provides a clear understanding of what normal is, and how to understand deviations from normal.
  - Trend Analysis
    Through the VM program in conjunction with the patch management capability process, is the organization getting better or worse over time?
  - Mean Time to Resolution
    Time from the discovery of the vulnerability to remediation. Measuring mean time to resolution allows the organization to gauge the applicability of its vulnerability policy and standards especially with regard to critical and high-risk items.
  - Vulnerability Age
    Measuring the age of the vulnerabilities in the vulnerability repository for tracking vulnerability life cycle and patch management cadence. The longer a vulnerability lives in an environment the more likely it will be used against you.

While most scanning solutions provide out-of-the-box metrics and reporting it is important to understand the basis for development of the organization's metric needs. First and foremost, determine who the stakeholders will be. A good place to start is with the executive team. What is important to an executive may be different to a technical stakeholder but understanding those data points drives discussion and decision making down through the VMP and across the connective tissue.

---

[8] Jack Freund and Jack Jones (2014), *Measuring and Managing Information Risk: A FAIR Approach*, 2014 Butterworth-Heinemann; 1st edition.

- Correlation

  The last point in vulnerability management is tied to correlation. A single vulnerability on a single asset may be a significant risk to the organization dependent on the criticality of the asset, the placement of the asset, and compensating controls. A single vulnerability across all assets in an organization may significantly raise the risk to the organization. Knowing that the SOC is seeing an increased traffic against the organization on, let's say, the port identified in the vulnerability or using a signature created for the vulnerability may signal a significant security incident. Correlating with all of the connective tissue, such as capabilities under the security operations oversight domain, will provide identification of events and prevent incidents through sharing of information.

  Correlation in vulnerability management has many layers and is driven through by the overall maturity of the CI-DR. In the lower end of the maturity scale, interaction with Security Operations Oversight is great place to start. In the higher end of the maturity scale there are technological solutions that orchestrate feeds from the vulnerability repository, network paths, and the threat landscape to name a few, and derive correlation to determine risk. This orchestration can be very helpful for organizations to determine the applicability, likelihood, and impact of identified threats.

- Vulnerability Management Team

  A VM program requires the underpinning of a robust team. Vulnerability management necessitates technical, security, and business acumen in conjunction with risk management knowledge and experience. The chosen team members will need to understand all aspects of an organization to be able to understand the technical details of vulnerabilities as well as be able to speak in a manner that the stakeholders of the organization can understand so they can make informed decisions.

  Based upon the size and maturity of an organization the VM program may be a single resource, or in the case of the real example I used previously, may be over a dozen. Choosing the right resources becomes more of a critical need as an organization grows and matures. Building any capability can be daunting in its execution and as such having a reference framework can provide a significant roadmap to success.

  The NIST Special Publication 800-181: National Initiative for Cybersecurity Education (NICE) Cybersecurity Workforce Framework provides a foundational overview on development of your cybersecurity workforce: "The NICE Framework supports those in the cybersecurity field and those who might wish to enter the cybersecurity field, to explore Tasks within cybersecurity Categories and work roles. It also assists those who support these workers, such as human resource staffing specialists and guidance counselors, to help job seekers and students understand which cybersecurity work roles and which associated Knowledge, Skills, and Abilities are being valued by employers for in-demand cybersecurity jobs and positions."[9]

The framework breaks job skills down into specific categories and then specialty areas like the vulnerability assessment and management (VAM), which aligns with the VMP:[10]

Categories	Descriptions
Securely Provision (SP)	Conceptualizes, designs, procures, and/or builds secure information technology (IT) systems, with responsibility for aspects of system and/or network development.
Operate and Maintain (OM)	Provides the support, administration, and maintenance necessary to ensure effective and efficient information technology (IT) system performance and security.
Oversee and Govern (OV)	Provides leadership, management, direction, or development and advocacy so the organization may effectively conduct cybersecurity work.
Protect and Defend (PR)	Identifies, analyzes, and mitigates threats to internal information technology (IT) systems and/or networks.
Analyze (AN)	Performs highly-specialized review and evaluation of incoming cybersecurity information to determine its usefulness for intelligence.
Collect and Operate (CO)	Provides specialized denial and deception operations and collection of cybersecurity information that may be used to develop intelligence.
Investigate (IN)	Investigates cybersecurity events or crimes related to information technology (IT) systems, networks, and digital evidence.

[9] William Newhouse, Stephanie Keith, National Initiative for Cybersecurity Education (NICE) Cybersecurity Workforce Framework, US Department of Commerce, https://doi.org/10.6028/NIST.SP.800-181.
[10] Source: https://doi.org/10.6028/NIST.SP.800-181.

The major categories described above provide an institution to derive VM team members, as the VM team composition relies on knowledge of all of the categories in its connectivity. At a more granular level key specialty areas to consider based upon the organization include but are not limited to:

- Vulnerability Assessment and Management (VAM)
- Risk Management (RSK)
- Network Services (NET)
- Systems Administration (ADM)
- Cyber Operations (OPS)
- Software Development (DEV)
- Systems Architecture (ARC)
- Systems Development (SYS)
- Systems Administration (ADM)

While the above framework provides a starting point, identification of the needs of the team should be based on the maturity of the technological makeup of the organization. Understanding the composition of the team members will provide guidance on the structure of the team. The structure of the team should be developed to meet the needs of the stakeholders. A typical midsize VM team may include but is not limited to:

- Vulnerability Tech
  Schedules, scans, and provides reports
- Vulnerability Analyst
  Analyzes and risk rates vulnerabilities based upon the vulnerability analysis process
- Project Manager
  Manages coordination with stakeholders for remediation
- Subject Matter Experts (SMEs)
  Experts with knowledge of the underlying system, for example, developers, sysadmins, network administrators, etc.

The team, its composition, and makeup are critical to successfully implementing a VM program. Technology can go a long way, but it is the people who drive the technology that drives a successful program.

NOTES

- Vulnerability management's connective tissue has been discussed in previous chapters: it is emphasized by having its own chapter to demonstrate the value for making decisions.
- A VM program integrated in the CI-DR program can assist in predicting potential operational outages.
- A VM program integrated in the CI-DR program can assist in providing in "near-real-time" criticality ratings for assets.

CHAPTER TEN

CI-DR™ Key Capability Incident Response Teams

By Dr. Steven Johnson

A fundamental principle is never to remain completely passive, but to attack the enemy frontally and from the flanks, even while he is attacking us. We should, therefore, defend ourselves on a given front merely to induce the enemy to deploy his forces in an attack on this front.

– Carl von Clausewitz

NCIDENT RESPONSE is the basic ability for an organization to prepare, detect, and respond to cyber events. Most executives understand the need and importance of a well-rehearsed incident response plan; most underestimate the value a well-functioning incident response program can bring to the organization's overall risk management practice. This chapter will focus on establishing an integrated incident response program, supporting ongoing risk management activities and pivoting from a reactive to a proactive offensive tool for managing cybersecurity risks. Cyber threat intelligence becomes the leveraged unit to make this all happen. Before we begin to make this reframing, it is important to understand the traditional role an incident response team plays within an enterprise organization and the shortcomings with limiting yourself to a simple reactive utility.

It may seem obvious but in fact too many organizations fail to establish an incident response capability until it is too late. The time to establish an incident response function is not at the time of incident discovery; great care and thought should go into preparing for incident response long before incident occurrence. Take caution in undervaluing the need for a well-trained incident response function; during an active cyber incident, risk to an organization is determined by the organization's ability to detect (shorten time of attack) and to respond (restoration of business operations).

A legacy approach to cybersecurity is to implement protections and control measures to "prevent" cybersecurity incidents from occurring. This is no longer a viable strategy. A one-dimensional defensive cybersecurity operation exposes an organization to being protected only against the threat vectors they have willingly known and planned for. Incident response teams can be unintentionally marginalized because they are seen as a necessary but less used component of a technology organization.

Incident response teams, coupled with cyber threat intelligence, can help to pivot an organization from a reactive (defensive) to a proactive (offensive) cyber operation. A great first step in making this a reality is with a robust security incident response team (SIRT). Let me be clear: transitioning a cyber operation to include offensive countermeasures is not as glamorous as the phrase might suggest. It is also not an open remit to begin active offensive measures (e.g. offensive hack operations). As the old adage goes – sometimes the best defense is a good offense. In terms of cybersecurity this may indicate a shift toward actively finding exposures, rehearsing response procedures, and conducting cyber range exercises, which will pivot an organization from waiting for something to happen and responding to looking for things which are happening and mitigating.

Having an embedded SIRT team to include forensics, incident response, and cyber threat intelligence is my preferred method of establishing a cohesive incident response function. Establishing certain functions is going to be influenced by your own organization's constructs, resourcing, level of regulation – and if you're doing it holistically – by your organization's cyber risk posture. For example, I often see elements of a firm's Security Operations Center (SOC) incorporated into response teams – disciplines such as vulnerability management (VM) or security logging and monitoring. You may choose to have stand-alone but closely connected SIRT and SOC teams working side by side. In smaller organizations the SIRT team may be a subcomponent of an in-house or outsourced Security Operations Center. I will leave it to you and your organization to determine which approach is best; the critical takeaway here is the need for close association with forensic and cyber threat intelligence as a pivot to proactive incident management.

Offensive incident management is the practice of combining incident preparation activities with cyber intelligence informed simulation. Offensive incident management drills require the capability to employ live simulation exercises with informed threat intelligence to not only respond and recover but also enhance defensive security posture during the recovery phase, not afterwards. Offensive incident management ups the response game and is intended to consider complex attack vectors such as insider threat and to protect an organization from exposure to lateral movement. At the core of an offensive incident management construct is the need, during an incident, to look beyond the impacted asset, business, environment, etc., and to think more broadly about likely threat actors, their motives, and tools, techniques, and procedures (TTPs). Just as an organization might employ a red team, blue team, or purple team construct to their VM programs – a similar construct, which I will define later, may also be used.

Perhaps nothing is more important in executing successful incident response than determining an incident response framework. An incident response framework defines the expected entry conditions, lifecycle, and containment criteria an organization expects when invoking incident response. I mention explicitly entry conditions. Entry conditions are the elemental characteristics which turn a cyber *event* into a cyber *incident*. It is important to make the distinction between event and incident. Too often I have seen organizations mired down by confusion between these two terms. As I mentioned within the chapter on forensics, within cyberspace lexicon matters.

The confusion, I believe, between cyber incident response and non-incident events stems from traditional IT problem management. It is undeniable there is a cross-pollination between information security divisions and information technology groups. In many organizations the chief information security officer (CISO) reports to a chief technology officer (CTO) or chief information officer (CIO), who are typically familiar with the practice of IT problem and incident management. In the traditional practice, IT problems generate IT incidents, which are then triaged with break/fix IT teams (infrastructure, platform, database teams, etc.). In the context of cybersecurity, the notion of "problem" is not recognized. Instead, when monitoring cyberspace, we are presented with "events" that generate "incidents." Because the CIOs and CTOs to whom the CISO reports are familiar with the concept of problems leading to incidents, CISOs are sometimes forced into ambiguity between what constitutes an event and what is the threshold for an incident.

It is not uncommon for an organization to have many multiples of events over incidents. It may also be possible that an organization may go many months between cyber incidents based upon the nature of complexity and level of exposure of an organization's assets. This underscores the need for a predefined incident framework taxonomy. In this perspective the incident framework taxonomy serves to support the mission of the incident response program while also establishing clear rules of engagement.

I mentioned previously many incident response teams are embedded within an SOC; this is not by mistake or convenience. Colocating the SOC function (which is charged with monitoring and correlation activities across the sensor grid) and the incident response function (which is charged with respond-and-recover activities) nets a benefit of establishing synergies between the frontline and the response function to aid in rapid detection, response, and recover activities. Again, when talking within the context of incident response, risk to an organization is reduced or increased based upon the efficiency to contain and recover.

When thinking more broadly the ability to detect is also important; however, I view this as "left of bang" or pre-incident, and not a bona fide function of incident response. An organization's ability to detect cyber intrusions and the like is important and a broad discussion around establishing an SOC, sensor grid, and analytics program could be had on its own. However, the word "response" implies the incident has already been detected and as such we will keep the conversation to "right of bang."

Myriad incident response framework taxonomies exist. Some frameworks have been created by security services vendors and consultancies, some by government organizations and regulators, and still other industry sectors have proposed cyber incident response frameworks that can be adopted. It is my experience that it is a bit difficult to outright adopt an incident response framework without some adaptation to suit the needs of your organization. If the organization is subject to certain regulatory oversight, adopt a modified framework derived from the regulator. If an industry or sector-specific framework, such as healthcare, offers some which can be leveraged, go for it. The key takeaway here is to not be shortsighted in adopting a framework wholesale without molding it to fit the needs of an organization. Not taking this extra step will almost certainly leave you scratching your head when you need to invoke incident response because it is not framed for the nuance of your operational environment. As this text is not industry or sector-specific, and does not endorse any one framework per se, we will discuss a basic lifecycle approach, which includes the major incident components of:

- Respond
- Contain
- Recover

It is my belief that an organization's ability to respond is correlated to its ability to prepare. I know you're thinking, "But you just said we are going to focus on right of bang." This is true; however, a lack of planning for incidents to occur likely will contribute to an ability to quickly respond. The transition between event and incident is the moment at which an organization invokes incident response. Let's examine this more closely.

From my point of view the primary differentiator between an event and an incident is determined by the level of impact an event has on an organization. In simple terms every incident could be an event and every event could be an incident. What is required is an established threshold and criteria for moving between monitoring and responding to events and raising the alarm of incident. Again, this transition should be rooted in impact.

Take, for example, malware; all organizations should employ the use of an endpoint antivirus product. These products, depending on their sophistication, can provide either static or dynamic malware protection. Static malware protection is the traditional signature-based antivirus. With signature-based antivirus the endpoint protection software is preloaded with a list of "signatures" (often a hash value or similar). The antivirus does its job by monitoring the endpoint for the presence of malicious binaries (malware) based on that file's signature. The limitation of static or signature-based protection tooling is the software can only protect against malware it knows about. This requires an organization to be diligent with providing ongoing updates to the antivirus malware definition or signature libraries. Even, when organizations are diligent with updating their endpoint protection software, the tooling is only as good as what it is asked to protect against.

Endpoint protection software, which incorporates dynamic monitoring and protection capabilities based on a behavioral approach, helps address the deficiency posed by static malware protection tools. Behavioral-based antivirus leverages heuristics (behavioral analysis) to determine if a binary is malicious or not. Many approaches exist to behavioral-based malware protection; however, they are quite basic in concept (quite a bit more difficult in approach). Behavioral-based antivirus will monitor the behavior of a system, the network activity, how applications are interacting with each other, and the system level – some even monitor and examine memory.

As you can imagine, the volume of processes which dynamic malware tools need to inspect and take a decision upon is immense. Signature-based malware tools have a very high confidence rating when detecting malware based upon its signature – the signature is the "tell" that will give the malware away. With behavioral-based malware antivirus, the tooling has to decide, some number of which will be a "false positive," requiring further investigation by an SOC analysis, for example. In an attempt to cut down the number of false positive alerts most manufacturers of behavioral-based antivirus will also incorporate signature-based capability. Nonetheless, when using behavioral-based antivirus it is expected to then have a capability which can review the alerts and decisions.

In the example given above, and for the purpose of incident response, we can equate alerts generated by antimalware and endpoint protection tools to cyber events. Events need to be cataloged, correlated, and analyzed. This correlation and analysis activity is a primary function of an SOC. As you might imagine, for a relatively large enterprise organization with twenty or thirty thousand people, the SOC receives a massive volume of alerts across the entire sensor grid and tool suite. For another day, but important to note, most organizations of this magnitude employ a security event and information monitoring (SEIM) platform. The SEIM is essentially a large repository which will consume alerts generated by your cybersecurity controls, normalize, and harmonize the data for analysis. Most SEIM products allow for basic correlation techniques, such as weighting the criticality of a particular alert to more advanced features like automation and orchestration.

Now that we have drawn a distinction between events and incidents we can pivot to determining an incident has occurred. When selecting and establishing an incident response framework, consideration should be given to key elements that might seem obvious at first but play a significant role in the ability to execute an incident response plan (more on that later). When establishing an incident response framework, it is best to begin with codifying the intended outcomes. What is incident response and what purpose is it attempting to fulfill? Seems obvious, right?

Call it expected outcomes, success criteria, mission statement, or whatever is going to communicate the purpose (and remit) the incident response function has. Purpose and remit are different. Purpose is the context by which incident response success and failure are measured. Purpose leads to mission objectives and objectives can be translated into measurable key performance indicators (KPIs). Remit is slightly different wherein there is a transition or assumption of authority (typically from executive management) to perform the incident response function. As with forensics, proper authorization to carry out incident response activities is necessary.

Purpose and remit are the foundation for establishing clear incident response roles and responsibilities. Roles and responsibilities should be predefined so the folks who are required to participate in incident response activities are aware of their expected contributions. Roles and responsibilities also help execute preparedness exercises and assess the effectiveness of response during an actual incident as a component of a postmortem.

I'd suggest capturing roles and responsibilities in a simple RACI matrix. RACI is an acronym for **R**esponsible **A**ccountable **C**onsulted and **I**nformed. A RACI matrix is a graphical representation of who leads what, contributes to what, and needs to be abreast of what. When an incident is declared emotions run high, many people may be engaged, and confusion can quickly ensue. A well-defined RACI matrix can help alleviate some of this ambiguity. When considering the people (or functions) involved in incident response and their expected participation, broaden your approach beyond technology and include representation from nontechnology business units. Depending on the nature and structure of your organization, nontechnology business units might be the Executive Office (CEO), Corporate Communications, Human Resources, Legal, Compliance, Privacy, Physical Security, Vendor Management, product or client-facing business leadership, and any third-parties such as service providers, internet service providers (ISPs), or managed security services provider (MSSPs). This broadly covers the requisite stakeholders to support your incident response activities.

Up to this point in the journey to establish an adequate incident response framework, we have mentioned the incident response lifecycle, events vs. incidents, roles and responsibilities, and key stakeholders. We can now turn our focus to the substance: procedures. I prefer the term *run book* or *playbook*. "Procedure" emits a bit of a mundane connotation for my liking, as procedures can be synonymous with corporate bureaucracy. When you inform the CISO you have invoked incident response and are triaging the incident pursuant to the DDoS playbook – it adds a level of gravitas needed to execute quickly and efficiently (DDoS by the way is a distributed-denial-of-service attack – most definitely an incident!).

Incident playbooks can take on many forms but only one function – to facilitate an adequate response to mitigate risk. Early in the days of cybersecurity incident response playbooks were literally bound documents, which had operational and sequenced response activities. Today most software-based incident response or ticketing systems have the capability to digitize the bound paper playbooks of the mid-2000s. Orchestration was mentioned above – orchestration takes the digital playbook a step further to software-enabled response. With orchestration, a software tool can execute rudimentary incident response triage activity without human intervention. For example, if you have an intrusion detection system (IDS) that has identified a laptop on the network, which might be infected with malware because the system's network activity looks suspiciously like command-and-control server activity, orchestration software might be able to consume the event alerting coming from your IDS system and through automation drop the system from your network.

However you instantiate your incident response playbooks (and I would still suggest keeping some physical copies handy), most playbooks should have some basic content which can then be tailored for the incident type at hand.

When structuring an incident response playbook, I find it best to include, at the forefront, basic information about the firm's incident management escalation processes. Information such as distribution lists, call trees, core contacts, and the like will be required in each incident management execution. Having this information readily available with clear instructions on how to use or initiate the incident declaration will save time and reduce confusion.

Declaring an incident is a significant responsibility; having basic criteria on what type of incident to declare is the next most important element of your incident response playbook. As part of your incident response framework it is ideal to devise some basic incident classifications or categories in which to thematically group your response efforts. This could be used for reporting purposes (e.g. metrics around incident type) or could be used to tailor the response participants and approach based on a predetermined strategy. A mechanism to account for severity or priority is a good idea as well. It is not uncommon to see parallel incidents being triaged at the same time. In many cases there may be primary, secondary, or tertiary response teams resolving multiple incidents at once. By implementing a prioritization mechanism (e.g. high, medium, low priority) the incident manager or coordinator will be able to choreograph the best response. Declaring an incident can be tumultuous; if you design declaration or "entry condition" for each incident type as a component of your incident management playbook or within your orchestration tool, doing so will decrease the likelihood of a false alarm or finger pointing.

A moment on nomenclature here – the phrase "entry condition" is derived from a military context; in cyberspace I like to have designated and pretested conditions which separate event from incident. Using a simple malware infection as an example: one or a handful of endpoints infected with a drive-by type malware with minimal overall impact to the organization is going to garner much less concern than if a system that houses the firm's financial statements was infected with the same. In this light example, a few employees will be inconvenienced for a half day while the end user support team collects their laptops and re-images them before returning to use. Whereas a system holding the firm's books and ledgers raises a more significant alarm; using the concept of impact and priority a few laptops used by employees is less of a concern than a critical firm system. Although the count is only one system I would likely declare the malware event on the financial statements system an incident and leave the routine employee malware events as events.

Through the use of entry conditions, decision trees, incident invocation criteria, and the like you effectively remove the declaration guesswork from the incident manager to a predetermined set of criteria. A basic approach to establishing incident criteria is through system type; most firms have a mechanism to classify their systems (usually based on criticality). It may make sense to establish a "crown jewel" or top criticality wherein validated alerts and events would invoke incident response simply based on the overall criticality, value, and thus importance to the firm. In the basic example given above, if we assumed the firm's ledger system to be a crown jewel system, invoking incident response would be an easy, if not expected, action given the entry condition to the malware response playbook indicated all crown jewel systems infected with malware establishes the need for incident declaration.

Making the leap from event to incident, to incident declaration we are now in a position to execute the response. We will talk more about tactically executing incident response below; sticking to the development of an incident playbook documenting the expected response actions is what's needed next. As with any type of emergency (say, fire or medical) there are always first responders.

Just as a paramedic in the field cannot administer full medical capabilities as a hospital can, the cyber first responder is limited in ability and the playbook should account for this. It might be interesting to note that many SOC orchestration tools fulfill the role of first responder, i.e. the basic actions that can be taken to reduce the escalation of the incident at hand.

A well-crafted incident playbook will recognize the fact that the initial first responder may not be the incident commander or even an individual from the incident response team. A first responder might be someone from the business, someone from another part of technology, a vendor, or even a customer. For this reason, a playbook should start with basic steps toward mitigation any individual could fulfill. This is usually codified as escalation paths through a hotline, ticketing system, or other communications channel. It also incorporates basic details that should be captured to contextual: the who, what, when, and where (oftentimes captured within the body of an incident ticket). Finally, based upon the incident type there may be some basic instructions for the reporting or discovering persons to execute in order to limit further damage.

The basic principle here is to have an initial set of instructions to quickly escalate the incident at hand and capture incident details, which will be important for triage and recovery. Many organizations will choose to post first responder–type details on their intranet, wiki pages, and even organizational policies, standards, and procedures. Whatever the approach taken, it is important to assume the likely user of the incident response playbook might not be a technical subject matter expert.

Lack of communications capabilities and the ability to communicate quickly and efficiently is the one element that can inhibit incident response efficiency. Your organization should establish business and technical call trees to leverage as part of the incident declaration process but also during triage and recovery. Many of the individuals who are to be notified when an incident occurs will likely participate in the postmortem process as well; more to come on that. As with incident type and priority, it is my suggestion that your organization establish the same approach to communications and escalations.

When an incident is invoked people begin to act quickly and at times this quick-to-action approach also creates a situation of chaos. One such situation is where chaos arises through having too many cooks in the kitchen all on a conference line and trying to assert their perspectives, needs, and sometimes authority to close an incident out. Technologists are accused of speaking too much tech and businesspeople are too mired down by the details. While having input from stakeholders is important and delivering transparency through communications during an incident is as well, it is easy to see how twenty or thirty people on an incident call can be chaotic.

One approach I have experienced and subsequently implemented at several organizations is the notion of communications teams based upon need to resolve an incident. I have conceptualized this based on a simple platinum, gold, silver, and bronze team construct. The bronze team and conference line is reserved for the technologists and incident commanders to coordinate the containment and recovery strategy. The bronze team conference bridge is typically an open-looped line where triage teams can jump in and out or listen and contribute passively as the incident evolves. The silver team is comprised of middle-level management and is typically chaired by the CIO, CTO, or CISO depending on the nature of the incident. The silver call is where the strategic decisions are made and the impact analysis is conducted. Other members of the silver team would be the head(s) of any impacted business functions, legal, compliance, vendor management, corporate communications, and any outside third parties.

The gold call is reserved for executive management. This is where the CIO, CTO, or CISO who facilitated the silver call provides awareness to senior executive leadership. In this instance the gold call would include folks who commonly have the "C" in front of their corporate title. The CEO, COO, CFO, chief privacy officer, chief compliance officer, chief human resources officer, etc., would all be likely participants. You might be wondering, then, what would a platinum call be used for? In industries, such as financial services, where regulatory oversight exists, the platinum-level call would be reserved to engage with stakeholders for a heightened nature. Some incidents might require the engagement of law enforcement, I would reserve this for the platinum team. From time to time an incident might have an impact on a significant client or companies if your organization provides services. Platinum-level calls should be rarely used and should be the decision of the gold team to use. It would not be uncommon for a platinum call to have outside counsel present, investor representatives, and recorded and secure lines used and be heavily scripted or rehearsed.

I find the bronze, silver, gold, and platinum construct to be the most efficient to implement. Not every incident response requires the use of each level. Depending on the severity and impact an incident has on an organization it might be perfectly acceptable to leverage a bronze and silver team communications construct with a situational awareness report (SITrep) via email to executive management. Balance is the key here and engaging only the organizational resources necessary to provide an adequate response and recovery. Do your best to avoid the "keen" executive from skip-leveling down from the gold to silver or bronze lines. Certainly, if there is value to have them there, by all means do it. Unfortunately, I have seen teams fall victim to the CIO who "rose through the ranks" and incidents are unnecessarily over-escalated to the top of the command chain when an incident could have easily been resolved more locally. The table below summaries the core elements behind the bronze, silver, gold, and platinum construct.

Level	Participants	Frequency
Platinum	■ Regulators ■ Law Enforcement ■ Shareholders ■ Clients / Customers ■ Vendors & Other Third Parties	As needed
Gold	■ Chaired by the CIO / CTO / CISO ■ CEO ■ COO ■ CFO ■ Chief Privacy Officer ■ Chief Compliance Officer ■ Chief Human Resources Officer ■ etc.	High impact incidents: ■ Every 2 hours by email ■ Every 3 hours via phone conference Medium impact incidents: ■ Every 3–4 hours via email ■ Every 6–12 via phone conference Low impact incidents: ■ Every 6 hours via email ■ Every 12–24 hours by phone conference (optional)
Silver	■ Chaired by the incident commander ■ CIO / CTO / CISO ■ Impacted stakeholders ■ Recovery stakeholders (compliance, privacy, legal, HR, etc.)	High impact incidents: ■ Every 1 hour by email ■ Every 2 hours via phone conference Medium impact incidents: ■ Every 2 hours via email ■ Every 3–6 via phone conference Low impact incidents: ■ Every 3–6 hours via email ■ Every 12–24 hours by phone conference (optional)
Bronze	■ Coordinated by the incident commander ■ Chaired by the team / person / unit which is accountable for executing the response and recovery actions	High and Medium impact incidents: ■ Open-loop conference bridge ■ Ongoing email / chat / slack / collaboration threads Low impact incidents: ■ Call bridge optional ■ Ongoing email / chat / slack / collaboration threads

All well-planned playbooks inevitably seem to fall short in predicting or prescribing response for all incident scenarios. While the aim of a playbook should be to codify the guiding principles a response team should follow it should not be overly prescriptive. Unless you have the tooling in place to script precise response actions or a particular response requires important sequencing details, try to avoid the desire to provide a respond-and-recovery "how-to." Testing, rehearsing, and exercising the playbook (we cover this at the end of the chapter) will help expose any playbooks which may be too directive.

Cyber threat intelligence enhances the ability for an organization to contain the impact of an incident through the application of curated knowledge about likely attacks and adversaries. Throughout this book we have presented ideas on how the use of cyber threat intelligence can enhance all aspects of a firm's cybersecurity program. While the majority of these recommendations are tailored to proactive and protective measures, it is during incident response where the task now becomes offensive and thus the phrase "offensive incident management."

Offensive not in the sense that when incident response is invoked we become the attackers, but in the sense that during incident response the organization is on the "back foot" so to speak. Leveraging cyber threat intelligence early in the incident response lifecycle will better enable an organization to return to a "neutral" footing or in some instances thrust an organization onto its "front foot." Cyber threat intelligence is a core component to ensuring this transition from back foot forward occurs.

Incident response is inherently reactive. Something has occurred which has changed the expected state of an operational environment which requires triage and remediation. The intent of this text is not to provide a robust examination of triage and containment strategies. A voluminous text could be written, and some have been, on this topic which could then be used as an informal how-to to incident containment. Instead, the focus of this book is to frame various competencies in the context of risk management and the use of cyber threat intelligence in supporting risk management practices.

In the context of incident response, cyber threat intelligence is best leveraged during preparation and containment. When preparing for incidents cyber threat intelligence can be employed to influence the type of scenario exercises chosen for rehearsal. It can also be used to influence the development of incident response playbooks; if an organization has a deterministic threat landscape with known threat actors and TTPs – plan for it.

Traditional approaches to incident response would dictate that a quick and efficient recovery is the most important aspect of incident response. It is important. However, if an organization transitions too quickly between contain and recover, valuable information might be lost. The application of cyber threat intelligence helps to ensure this is not the case.

Cyber threat intelligence has the potential to influence the containment strategy. Thinking back to our earlier malware example, it is quick and efficient to pull machines from the network, re-image, and then redeploy back into service. Incident triaged and remediated. Remediated, yes, in the sense an incident is no longer active but not in the very real sense the organization is likely still vulnerable to exactly the same threat vectors. If cyber threat intelligence were to be employed in our basic example, an organization might then have the ability to pivot forward to understand some basic questions:

- What does the malware do?
- How did we become compromised?
- Where within the cyber kill chain are we?
- Who or what attribution can be made?

Cyber threat intelligence may facilitate the answering of these basic questions although the answers are not required to actually triage and recover from an incident. On face value these questions posed seem a bit rudimentary. Some may argue they are "nice to haves" and not needed and this is likely true. However, in the context of risk management, without having the ability to provide a basic response to each of the questions posed, the organization will likely remain exposed to the exact same attack or compromise and will have little ability to effectively assess its control design and effectiveness. If the focus of incident response is simply an ability to close incident tickets, then, yes, pivoting quickly from detection to closure will be top priority.

If the primary focus of incident response is to reduce risk to your organization, then offensive incident response supported by an effective cyber threat intelligence program is right for you. Cyber threat intelligence during incident containment can provide more than just attribution or knowing who might have attacked or exploited your organization. Cyber threat intelligence can also provide critical assessment, in real time, to be incorporated in your active incident impact assessment. Similar to the entry conditions for invoking incident response, an ongoing incident impact assessment will enable you as the incident commander to adequately assess your state of triage and recovery.

During an incident the focus is recovering from the exposure at hand; when leveraged, cyber threat intelligence can also be used to ensure the incident is less likely to reoccur. By employing cyber threat intelligence alongside an ongoing incident recovery, the intelligence team can coordinate an assessment of the attack vectors across the remainder of the organization. In our malware example, having an intelligence summary on the exploited weakness and assessing other critical assets with similar exposure enables me to understand my maximum potential impact zone.

Additionally, we can take the threat assessment further in that knowledge of the attack vectors by assessing our current control suite design and effectiveness to aid in identifying secondary or tertiary weaknesses not yet exploited. Lateral movement within an enterprise should always be a consideration when dealing with incidents where there is a potential of network intrusion. A cyber threat intelligence team, in tandem with the recovery efforts, could complete an attack tree analysis to help identify potential east–west movement.

Attack tree analysis is a mechanism based on graph theory, which allows a threat assessment based on system connectivity, controls, and target value. Attack tree analysis enables a cyber threat analysis starting from the exploited system down to a high-value target. Starting at the edge, an intelligence analyst would then determine interconnected systems; in between these interconnected systems lies a control suite. Access controls, network routing constraints, APIs security, and database security controls are examples of likely controls that inhibit free lateral movement. The analyst can rate the effectiveness of each control between systems (I like to use difficulty and time as basic variables), which would need to be overcome in order to make a movement.

The attack tree analysis continues until you have either run out of movements (good thing) or you've gained access to the high value you target (potentially bad thing). If you have reached your high-value target during analysis, you have in theory bypassed all of your preventative controls. If this occurs, pivot back up stream and assess the effectiveness of your detective controls (logging and monitoring). By leveraging cyber threat intelligence during incident response, you can understand attribution, your posture against likely reoccurrence, and the relative effectiveness of protections against other assets, but most importantly – a deterministic way of improving your risk profile once an incident is resolved.

Incident recovery has three core phases and cyber threat intelligence can be incorporated within each. The three phases of incident recovery are validation, postmortem and improvement. We will take each of these one at a time by defining them and stating the role cyber threat intelligence plays within each. Although I have broken recovery into three distinct phases they are not mutually exclusive, and each incident should not be deemed closed until each recovery phase has been completed.

Recovery validation is the basic notion that whatever triggering event invoked incident response has been remedied. This is ostensibly the "end" of the incident. In order to achieve incident validation, the response-and-recovery strategy should have been executed and either a temporary or permanent fix be in place. In the context of a cybersecurity incident the "fix" is typically a mitigating or compensating control either through enhancement of an existing control or something new altogether. Validation is only required against the impacted asset and the vector(s) exploited. Other systems may be vulnerable to the same attack; however, we will address this aspect in a moment.

Cyber threat intelligence is a fantastic utility to help assess and validate incident response activities. While the responding technology teams are in triage mode, the cyber threat analyst is researching and learning about what was compromised and how. This information should be fed in real time to the triage team but can also be leveraged to vet and affirm that the actions taken have addressed the realized risk against the impact systems. I also like to leverage the cyber threat intelligence team (coupled with my forensic capability) to provide a level of independent validation. The triaging technology teams are focused on recovery, wherein the intel and forensics team can act as an assurance function to the process.

Once the recovery actions have been validated the incident response team should transition to improvement. As with all things, not all attack vectors, scenarios, and threat actors can be planned for or mitigated. All organizations, regardless of size, are bound by limited time and resources. The improvement phase of recovery is designed to transpose the resolved incident across the remainder of the enterprise. In short, this is the moment where you come up for air and ask yourself what other assets might be exposed to this vulnerability or exposure? It is okay to run in parallel the validation and improvement phases; you might be wondering why even break them apart. Depending how well your incident response program is run, this obvious step to examine the remainder of the estate might not be so obvious. Time after time I have witnessed organizations respond and recover from an incident in a bit of a vacuum. This isn't intentional but is a result of decentralized technology management, siloed organizations, and sometimes simply lack of transparency. The resulting scenario is one where an incident occurs and is resolved only for the same incident to pop-up somewhere else in the organization. This is another aspect where cyber threat intelligence can bring value.

Leverage the cyber threat intelligence team to complete the organization-wide view. The intelligence team can even be utilized further in working with technology teams to move from temporary control implemented during incident response to a more strategic approach to mitigating the realized risk. The cyber intelligence team should also have an analysis of your organization's threat landscape and an alignment to likely high-value targets internally on which to prioritize your control improvement and investments. Simply put, the cyber threat intelligence team can be leveraged to ensure the vector exploited during an incident and the resulting response is adopted into the firm's cybersecurity control suite and adequately applied across all exposed assets.

The postmortem is the final stage in recovery and my preference is to make the postmortem process the least technical of all. The postmortem is an opportunity to blamelessly discuss the relevant facts and sequencing of events. I like to begin the postmortem process with a plain language incident executive summary and a succinct timeline of events. I find these two pieces alone drive a fact-based discussion between business and technical stakeholders with the intended output being after-action items for the incident response process. Notice I said, "incident response process." Many postmortems I've seen conducted lump the technical shortcomings (e.g. controls) with process failure. This is why I choose to break out improvement and postmortem into stand-alone elements. The postmortem should be reserved for talking with stakeholders about how the incident response process succeeded and how it might become quicker, better, faster.

Cyber threat intelligence, being a stakeholder in the incident response process, has a unique role to play in a process or business-oriented postmortem. Everything we do in cybersecurity has the singular mission to reduce risk. During a postmortem the cyber threat intelligence function can contribute to the risk assessment by contextualizing how the suffered risk event could have been worse (or better). An intelligence analyst can act as an independent voice to process breakdowns or sequencing issues. Cyber threat intelligence can also be used as a tool to forecast the return on any investments made as a result of the incident by completing a forward-looking impact assessment based on the incident reoccurring with or without proposed investments in place. It adds perspective to the investment ask and justifies the commercial investment versus the commercial impact.

You cannot talk about incident response without lightly addressing incident preparedness and the role cyber threat intelligence plays. Preparing for an incident should naturally occur before you find yourself in an incident response mode. Additionally, incident preparedness should immediately follow an incident postmortem, otherwise what is the point in completing the postmortem and associated after-action items?

Whether it be through the use of a tabletop exercise or a more advanced cyber range simulation, incident response exercises should not fall short by testing process alone. Wherever practical, the technological elements of your incident response toolkit (e.g. alerting, monitoring, and forensic capabilities) should be tested in parallel as well. Additionally, the preparedness exercises should be based in likely scenarios, otherwise you are wasting people's time. Cyber threat intelligence can act as the creators and facilitators of cyber range scenarios. When based on assessed threat actors and likely TTPs, a tabletop exercise can quickly be transformed in to a bit of a cyber war game which encompasses the full incident lifecycle with participation from technology and business alike. The output of such a high-quality scenario exercise should conclude with a response validation, improvement, and relevant postmortem to proactively (i.e. offensively) address cyber risk through a well-designed and organized incident response function.

 NOTES

- Incident response programs cannot just happen after an incident, they must be thoughtfully implemented and understood by business leaders.
- Business units should have representation in this capability; decisions will need to be made quickly and those decisions could impact operations, financials, regulatory, etc.
- Business leaders have to make decisions during incidents. The Incident Response program within the CI-DR provides for pre-decisions, guidance for continuity of operations, and the ability to contain and recover operations.

CHAPTER ELEVEN

CI-DR™ Collection Components

*Every age has its own kind of war, its own limiting
conditions, and its own peculiar preconceptions.*

– Carl von Clausewitz

C OLLECTING INFORMATION and gathering data is indispensable for
being able to build an effective CI-DR™ program. One area that we
need data from is independent testing teams that perform penetration
testing. *Penetration testing* comes in various maturity states and various reporting, sometimes as vulnerability assessment information, which only includes
possible vulnerabilities. Our CI-DR program works within the constraints of
the organization's willingness to perform deep testing and actual exploitation
activities similar to those done by cyber adversaries. We asked Mario DiNatale,
a practicing Whitehat and Expert Tester, with former and active roles as CTO,
CIO, and CISO, for his opinion on what is wrong with some of today's penetration testing activities and his thoughts on how the right data can change
decisions.

*It's quite often I hear my pen-testing work described as "Art." Or Voodoo.
Or Magic.*

Whilst flattering to hear, it's also dismaying, partly because it's confirmation that a client has been swindled by a pen-tester that came before me, but also because a good quality pen-test is truly formulaic science. It's all too often in this industry that I see clients utilizing big-name firms believing that this is what will yield them the best results. From the reports that have been shared with me, this is often not the case. I have literally seen pasted nmap scans or vulnerability scans handed in as reports to these clients and it's infuriating to continue to see this fraud continually perpetrated across the industry. Upon checking these vendors' websites, a common theme that set off red flags with me immediately (that if it hasn't with you, it should now) is that they had the gall to charge PER I.P.

When you're looking for a solid pen-test, you should be looking to hire a trusted adviser for 1–2 weeks of their time. Hiring a quality pen-tester is no different than hiring a qualified attorney or doctor. A pen-test that charges per I.P. is like typing your symptoms into Web MD and counting that as your yearly physical. As a trusted adviser, you're asking this person to use their intimate knowledge of systems and configurations to help you fortify your posture by testing your controls. A pen-test that uses pre-built tools and races to exploit devices and gain administrative level access is as useless as not having a pen-test in this regard. Your pen-tester should be able to speak with your team, align the test with your organization's goals and even emulate certain threat scenarios that you believe your organization may be vulnerable to. The tester should be able to run this tailored threat simulation for you and also provide a debrief session for your organization that thoroughly explains not only the attack path taken, but also their suggested remediations for helping your organization prevent this attack. This should be a collaborative session where the pen-tester is providing their expert knowledge of systems to help your team tailor fit a solution to the security flaws found that will be most applicable.

If the pen-test is simply being done for compliance reasons and the cheapest bid and the biggest name win the business, then that's fine. However, since you're spending money on a pen-test anyway, wouldn't it be better to derive actual value from the engagement?

Penetration testing activities should be viewed as a way to test the completeness of your controls and risk-mitigation technologies. As part of the security testing capability, penetration testing, physical security testing, and social engineering activities correlate into providing a collaborative and integrated CI-DR view of the security posture. Within the penetration testing concepts there fall testing of infrastructure, testing of physical protections, testing of applications, and testing of actual code. Data collected from these various testing principles can provide detail into determining how an adversary may operate within a network or system, should they be able to gain unauthorized access.

We mentioned quickly the importance of external threat feeds as we discussed the cyber threat intelligence capability. External threat feeds today differ completely from those five years ago. Today, those feeds can include current vendor cybersecurity assessments, dark and deep web key work or code snippet data; they also can include data from social media platforms or information about geopolitical activities occurring around the company's locations. LinkedIn is the dominant social networking site for professionals. In 2011, there were multiple instances of what are being referred to as virtual cyber spies. Multiple users reported a phishing expedition to identify and engage information operations (IO) experts and others on LinkedIn. They've reported invitations from an individual calling himself George W., who purports to be "Colonel Williams," an "IO professional" in the Washington DC area. Invitations, with a number of wording variations, have been received by a number of active-duty IO personnel recently. Investigation by several others has shown that the profile is for a nonexistent person. This is clearly the evolution of espionage and you can expect to see much more of this kind of activity from now on.[1]

External threat feeds can also be consumed based on industry, geolocation, particular systems (Windows, or Chrome, etc.), or as part of an anonymous feed of indicators of compromise (IOC) coming from one of the information sharing and analysis centers (ISACs) we mentioned earlier in the book. External threat feeds can seem to be overwhelming but in reality the digital nature of this data can live in systems designed for the collection, like a data lake or similar technologies. The data need not be normalized, but has to be collected from confident sources, without bias, and of course without the ability to be tampered with. Internal threat feeds will be even larger and will contain some very sensitive information.

▮ NOTES

- Coordination and Intelligence is the acquisition and analysis of information to identify, track, and predict cyber capabilities, intentions, and activities to offer courses of action that enhance decision-making.

---

[1] Kevin Colman, *Cyber Commander's Handbook*, Association for Computing Machinery, 2013 v 4.

- Improving the defense of a network requires a thorough understanding of what you are defending and defending against.
- Comprehensive information about the capabilities and intent of threat actors includes understanding their objectives and having details about their previous activities, tactics, techniques, procedures, and tools. This informs the development of effective countermeasures.
- Similarly, maintaining situational awareness of current vulnerabilities in an organization's networks, applications, operating environment, and sector creates a shared understanding of both the risks and mitigations.
- Organizations are able to determine a profile that best describes them, either by indications of targeted attacks or by cyber footprint.
- Organizations starting a new cyber intelligence function are able to identify/craft the objective for the function.
- Organizations are able to utilize the guidance on key competencies, skills, and traits of an intelligence analyst to craft job descriptions and hire analysts needed to support the cyber intelligence function.
- Organizations are able to utilize the guidance on leadership to identify and hire the best person to lead the cyber intelligence function.
- Organizations are able to utilize the guidance on analyst experience and tools and technical proficiencies to identify the most competent staff and the tools needed to support successful analysis.
- Organizations are able to determine the progression path of their cyber intelligence function and use the guidance provided to identify the leadership experience, analyst experience, tools, and technical proficiencies to advance their cyber intelligence capabilities.

CHAPTER TWELVE

CI-DR™ Stakeholders

By Steve Dufour, CEO

Many cyber vulnerabilities exist because of a lack of cybersecurity awareness on the part of computer users, systems administrators, technology developers, procurement officials, auditors, chief information officers (CIOs), chief executive officers, and corporate boards. Such awareness-based vulnerabilities present serious risks to critical infrastructures regardless of whether they exist within the infrastructure itself.

– Priority III: A National Cyberspace Security Awareness and Training Program

EXECUTIVES AND the board of directors are the primary consumers of the CI-DR™ analysis and "knowledge" reporting. Being a steward of the organization's financial, personnel, and business growth, it is invaluable to have all the facts during decision-making processes. Cyber today is the "silver bullet" that can disrupt or destroy an entire organization due to the inability to conduct operations, creating unexpected financial losses, or ultimately ruining the organization's reputation, leading to credit, market, liquidity, and capital losses.

In previous chapters we discussed the cyclical nature of the CI-DR programs and related processes, tool, tactics, and techniques and with each iteration of the process, the strategic intent is to create continual situational awareness and business impact context through the dissemination of recent and relevant cyber intelligence-based information. Senior corporate executives and the board of directors are the primary consumers of the CI-DR analysis and "knowledge" reporting but there are many internal and external stakeholders that contribute to and benefit from the CI-DR tactics, techniques, and procedures. The company executives, connected with the board of directors, are ultimately responsible for establishing, planning, and approving the risk management controls for the safeguarding of all company assets but it literally takes a village of internal and external key stakeholders to implement and continuously improve the organization's cyber readiness. The CI-DR processes and procedures are a balanced combination of technologies, tactics, technics, procedures, tools, and best practices for the collecting, processing, verifying, and exploitation and dissemination of cyber intelligence to be consumed by the company in the planning, organizing, directing, and controlling of day-to-day operations. Proper execution of the CI-DR program provides real-time cyber intelligence data to continually enable cybersecurity situational awareness and provides valuable input into all key business risk management decision-making processes. With proper execution of the CI-DR program it is possible to fuse business intelligence data with cyber and physical security data to truly enable "intelligence" to enhance organizational risk management decision-making processes on a real-time basis. See Figure 12.1

Positioning cyber intelligence to drive risk management can be the organizational "silver bullet" that can proactively avoid the disruption due to the inability to conduct operations. Today, many organizations still rely on the news, local media, cocktail party conversations, and hallway rumors passed through many of the social media channels which for various reasons create fear, uncertainty, and doubt (FUD) in the business community. Most of these conversations start with the "sky is falling" approach and a lot of technical

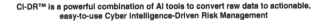

CI-DR™ is a powerful combination of AI tools to convert raw data to actionable, easy-to-use Cyber Intelligence-Driven Risk Management

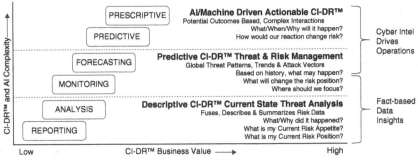

FIGURE 12.1 CI-DR and AI compatibility.

jargon that the cyber industry has created. This unreliable flow of unverified information should be discounted because, as you will have gathered from the previous pages, cyber is about business and the CI-DR program creates your own reliable, personal news with answers you need to continue with the management of business risk.

Think of what you may have read or heard in mainstream media about recent cyberattacks, and ask yourself how the reported cyber event could operationally impact how your organization conducts business. The CI-DR program has the capability to enable key stakeholders (boards, C-suite executives, managers, supervisors and employees, external auditors, etc.) to start with that list of important questions about the risk associated with cybersecurity and have the program answer the question with verifiable intelligence data. For example, a question could be asked about how malicious code placed in our critical system could adversely impact conducting business, and you would expect to hear back about the financial impacts, operational downtime, or a few options regarding resources or resiliency options. You do not want to be responded with a list of tools providing risk mitigation, or the number of vulnerabilities that critical system has; those answers provide no value to you in making decisions.

Of course, there are basic cybersecurity components that every organization should have as we discussed earlier, but what makes the application of the CI-DR program unique is your ability to document the risk appetites set by the executives and directors of each company, determine the current risk and threat levels in real-time, and ask questions to create situational awareness against stated business requirements. To properly establish and set those risk appetites there is a need for real-time, verified information, and the ability to direct pertinent questions at each department, group, division, or person. There will be times that risk will not be quantified or understood, and the decision will rely on organizational experience and wisdom, but with a proper CI-DR program the cyber risk can be added to enhance those experiences and lead to repeatable, predictable, or enhanced decision-making.

As a steward the need to ensure the organization is leveraging the CI-DR model for obtaining answers, collecting the right data, and using that knowledge to determine if those outcomes are within the risk appetite limits is a part of the modern toolkit for today's business and cyber leaders.

There are many internal and external stakeholders in the development and execution of the CI-DR program. With proper planning, implementation and training key stakeholders are instrumental to the flow of information and each stakeholder uses the output of the CI-DR to create a 360° view of the company's current risk and threat position. Figure 12.2 sets out a subset of the many key stakeholders and how they benefit from the implementation of the CI-DR program.

An effective CI-DR program is no longer a luxury; it is a business necessity. The CI-DR provides a constant stream of useful data and triggers when key indicators impacting organization risk are met. As the CI-DR program matures, it becomes the integrator between business operations, cyber operations, and risk management and compliance. Every key stakeholder in the enterprise will need to contribute to the knowledge base and will extract significant value at program inception through continuous improvement.

Another area that needs to be avoided is attempting to validate or compare the organization you are responsible for against a competitor or organization in a similar industry, which is a waste of resources, discussion, and leads to over-expenditures. Of course, there are basic cybersecurity components that every organization should have as we discussed earlier, but what makes your organization unique and your ability to determine risks is the risk appetite set by the executives and directors of each company. To set those risk appetites there is a need for information, and questions directed at each department, group, division, or person; as we discussed, those requests for information are similar to the military commanders' critical and priority intelligence requests. They are part of their decision-making process that impacts life-or-death situations.

Company Roles & Responsibilities	CI-DR Key Discussion Points
CEO, Senior Executive and Board of Directors	▪ The CI-DR Program starts and ends with the CEO, the Senior Executives and the Board of Directors ▪ This team must understand, assess and assume ultimate responsibility for organizational risk management that includes cybersecurity ▪ This team will have an easy to use, fact-based approach to creating actionable intelligence to measurably improve business risk decision-making processes ▪ This team establishes the business critical intelligence requirements, priorities, risk appetite and holds the CI-DR system for providing actionable intelligence to enhance the organization's risk decision-making processes
IT Professionals, Physical, DATA & Cyber Security Subject Matter Experts	▪ The CI-DR Program Designers, Implementors, Trainers & Maintainers ▪ Comprehensively integrated into the Cybersecurity Enterprise EcoSystem ▪ Seamlessly integrates the Cybersecurity EcoSystem into the business risk management decision-making processes ▪ This team establishes the common Information and Intelligence picture, and the common operating picture, and establishes the baseline for continuous understanding and situational awareness of the cyber threat against the risk management key registers
Risk Officers, Compliance Managers and Auditors	▪ The CI-DR Program's most valuable contributors, users and examiners of the actionable intelligence data ▪ This team establishes the organizational requirements for the CI-DR Program, the common information/intel picture, the common operating picture and the ultimate designers of the system logic and algorithmic components ▪ This internal and external team is responsible for the ultimate verification and certification of the actionable intelligence data outputs to the many users of this system ▪ They provide critical input and quality assurance that the CI-DR data structures are accurate, repeatable and predictable
Investor, Public & Media Relations, M&A Teams, Financial Institutions, etc.	▪ The CI-DR Program contemplates the requirements for the information needs of these key stakeholders and delivers key, timely data for the managers of these areas ▪ Any mistakes in these areas cause significant pain to the entire business; these areas are often included in the reactive response to a cyber threat but the CI-DR Program moves response from a reactive to a proactive communication position
Human Resource, Legal and Safety Compliance	▪ The CI-DR Program gathers internal and external data points and measures everything against stated requirements, compliance measures and corporate policies to assist in the development of business risk management ▪ These internal and often external teams contribute to the knowledge base, the collection of intel and the verification of the fact base

FIGURE 12.2 Benefits of key stakeholders.

As a steward, the need to ensure the organization is leveraging the CI-DR model for obtaining answers, collecting the right data, and using that knowledge to determine if those outcomes are within the risk appetite limits is a part of the toolkit for today's leaders. Leveraging the CI-DR model starts as mentioned previously, by requesting information from the leader of a particular department. For example, you are attempting to answer the question, "Is the organization confident that if there is a problem known early enough, we can adequately investigate, contain, minimize the damage, respond, recover, and mitigate the risk of reoccurrence?" Using the CI-DR model, a request to the risk officer (RO) for answers may be the first step in obtaining the knowledge necessary. The RO would then most likely request certain specific information from Operational Risk, Technology Risk, and Information Security if those departments and personnel exist. The CI-DR model feeds into the Operational Risk, as most operations today are digital in nature. Technology Risk feeds into the CI-DR and Information Security provides the missing or enhanced knowledge as this is where analysis occurs.

Our example in the introduction can be expanded further into the role of the Executive. There will be times that risk will not be quantified, and the decision will rely on your experience and wisdom, but with a proper CI-DR program the cyber risk can be added to enhance those experiences. For example, you, using our example, have received the analysis and data regarding the organization's overall loss expectancy for the example cyber event, and in your experiences you might not want to take the risk of losing any costs.

After the request of information is returned and evaluated by the RO, the executives would receive a briefing on the outcomes and key data points providing a full view of the organization with cyber included.

Similar to how they currently handle other issues of major strategic impact – such as marketplace uncertainty, regulatory complexity, or credit volatility – so must financial institutions manage cyber risks. They need to continually assess the scope and nature of their cyber landscape and create an integrated picture of their aggregate risk. They need to incorporate that picture into all relevant business decisions, both strategic and operational. They need to be deliberative about where they are willing to accept cyber risk, and where they are willing to invest to mitigate it. In short, they need to manage cyber risks as they do any other operational risks that can lead to major losses.

NOTES

- Stakeholders are the consumers and composers of the CI-DR program, as it was designed to bring cyber intelligence into operational risk and provide business decisions.
- Each stakeholder has different criteria and concerns. The CI-DR program acknowledges those differences and adapts reporting to meet those demands.

Conclusion

Be audacious and cunning in your plans, firm, and persevering in their execution, determined to find a glorious end.

– Carl von Clausewitz

T HE THREAT landscape in a cyber-connected world is changing fast. Technology continues to evolve at a rapid pace and new business models are rapidly adopting a heavily digitized global market. The physical boundaries of the past have fallen to a global market. As such, organizations must adapt to a new borderless security model that can adapt quickly to meet new business goals and objectives. The CI-DR™ framework is designed to take a company from having no cyber decision capabilities, to an integrated and mature program. We have provided the reader with the basics of what our CI-DR program should consist of, what is needed to make the connective tissue work within existing cybersecurity programs, and how those programs can be enhanced to connect cybersecurity to operational risk.

With the rapid expansion, organizations face not only increased threats, but threats from an ever-growing list of threat actors. Whether it is organized crime, state sponsored, insider threat, hacktivists, corporate competitors, or the indiscriminate hacker, organizations need to get ahead of the threats that pose risk to the business by identifying the intent, opportunity, and capability of the adversaries of the organization. I am sure the reader has heard that "cybersecurity" is the top business risk for many organizations. This is due to lower barrier to entry for adversaries, large-scale and impactful finanical gains for cyber adversaries, loss of talented leadership due to lack of understanding, and failure to perform basic cyber hygiene functions and continuing to buy new technologies that do not solve the problems at hand.

We provided the reader with real-world examples of how the CI-DR capabilities can support business leadership, support operational risk, and support purchasing of more thoughtful cyber technologies. CI-DR is not a fictious or intangible program, it has been proven and refined over the past 25 years, leveraging military experiences, operating and testing each capability within different organizations and within different industries. CI-DR is not easy, but once the first steps are taken the program will grow and evolve with the business. If you have already implemented the CI-DR framework, built your programs, or developed new technologies, we are sure you see the value in the way the connective tissue between capabilities and the interconnections between business leaders and cyber professionals have changed.

We also ask that those from the traditional military intelligence background look at the CI-DR program as a fork or stem that has evolved from the decades of work and lessons learned that has to be adapted for commercial usage. If there is a particular area where you as a reader feel that we inaccurately captured a military concept, please let us know and we can make those changes or explain in further detail our attempt at transforming that idea or concept. We hope you, the reader, leave with the understanding that the CI-DR program has a direct impact on business decisions and can proactively support risk mitigation strategies in an organization. It can also help provide the right framework for an organization that has yet to incorporate cyber intelligence operations into its cyber-security program and can be useful to reduce the following issues in an organization:

- An inability to identify sophisticated cyberattacks.
- Reacting to adverse events, not being able to predict them.
- Focusing only on what the organization sees on the network.
- Not being able to focus on the relevant information in the vast amounts of information the organization collects.
- An inability to align cyber threats to business risks.
- An inability to mature and refine the organization's capabilities to address the most relevant threats to the organization.
- Increased successful cyberattacks.

The indirect impact and risk to an organization that fails to incorporate cyber intelligence into its cybersecurity program can be but is not limited to:

- Higher cyber insurance rates
- Loss of market confidence (i.e. lower stock price, lower sales, etc.)
- Executive and board of directors' litigation (stockholders)
- Regulatory fines

We thank you for the time you took to read our book and look forward to all reviews; without them the CI-DR concepts never get nurtured to grow or provide new insight into what others are concerned about or what problems others are trying to solve.

Glossary

Asset   People, property, and information. People may include employees and customers along with other invited persons such as contractors or guests. Property assets consist of both tangible and intangible items that can be assigned a value. Intangible assets include reputation and proprietary information. Information may include databases, software code, critical company records, and many other intangible items.

Authenticity   Authenticity refers to the veracity of the claim of origin or authorship of the information. For example, one method for verifying the authorship of a handwritten document is to compare the handwriting characteristics of the document to a sampling of others which have already been verified. For electronic information, a digital signature could be used to verify the authorship of a digital document using public-key cryptography (could also be used to verify the integrity of the document).

Availability   Availability means having timely access to information. For example, a disk crash or denial-of-service attack both cause a breach of availability. Any delay that exceeds the expected service levels for a system can be described as a breach of availability.

Confidentiality   Confidentiality refers to limits on who can get what kind of information. For example, executives concerned about protecting their enterprise's strategic plans from competitors; individuals concerned about unauthorized access to their financial records.

Controls   These can be preventive, detective, or corrective, and can come in the form of administrative, logical, or physical-type controls.

  Administrative   These are the laws, regulations, policies, practices, and guidelines that govern the overall requirements and controls for an information security or other operational risk program. For example, a law or regulation may require merchants and financial institutions to protect and implement controls for customer account data to prevent identity theft. The business, in order to comply with the law or regulation, may adopt policies and procedures laying out the internal requirements for protecting this data, which requirements are a form of control.

Logical   These are the virtual, application, and technical controls (systems and software), such as firewalls, antivirus software, encryption, and maker/checker application routines.

Physical   Whereas a firewall provides a "logical" key to obtain access to a network, a "physical" key to a door can be used to gain access to an office space or storage room. Other examples of physical controls are video surveillance systems, gates, and barricades, the use of guards or other personnel to govern access to an office, and remote backup facilities.

Preventive   These are controls that prevent the loss or harm from occurring. For example, a control that enforces segregation of responsibilities (one person can submit a payment request, but a second person must authorize it) minimizes the chance an employee can issue fraudulent payments.

Detective   These controls monitor activity to identify instances where practices or procedures were not followed. For example, a business might reconcile the general ledger or review payment request audit logs to identify fraudulent payments.

Corrective   Corrective controls restore the system or process back to the state prior to a harmful event. For example, a business may implement a full restoration of a system from backup tapes after evidence is found that someone has improperly altered the payment data.

Crown Jewels   Crown jewels come in a few different varieties, physical jewels, intellectual property, and technology. We define "technology crown jewels" as the most valuable application(s) and/or system(s) used in decision making overall for the company (e.g. Coca-Cola's secret recipe). Technology crown jewels have specific characteristics of profitability, asset value, and future prospects and are measured by their asset value, earning power, and business prospects. Examples of technology crown jewels can be any level of data classification whereby intellectual property, customer ID information, and financial records are stored, transmitted, or processed; and where a breach, outage, or loss would severely diminish the company's finances and reputation. Loss may result in heavy fines and/or jail time.

CWE   Common Weakness Enumeration (CWE™) is a community-developed list of common software and hardware weakness types that have security ramifications. "Weaknesses" are flaws, faults, bugs, vulnerabilities, or other errors in software or hardware implementation, code, design, or architecture that if left unaddressed could result in systems, networks, or hardware being vulnerable to attack. The CWE List and associated classification taxonomy serve as a language that can be used to identify and describe these weaknesses in terms of CWEs.[1]

Deprived Value Deprival value is based on the premise that the value of an asset is equivalent to the loss that the owner of an asset would sustain if deprived of that asset. It builds on the insight that often the owner of an asset can use an asset to derive greater value than that which would be obtained from an immediate sale. For example, a machine may be profitably employed in a business but no more than scrap value could be obtained from its sale (net selling price).

Deprival value reasons that the maximum value at which an asset should be stated is its replacement cost as, by definition, the owner can make good the loss arising from deprival by incurring a cost equivalent to replacement cost. However, if that amount is greater than the amount that can be derived from ownership of the asset, it should be valued at no more than its recoverable amount. Recoverable amount is in turn defined as the higher of net selling price and value in use, which is the present value of the future returns that will be made by continuing to use the asset.

Infrastructure as a Service (IaaS) Infrastructure as a Service is a provision model in which an organization outsources the equipment used to support operations, including storage, hardware, servers, and networking components. The service provider owns the equipment and is responsible for housing, running, and maintaining it. The client typically pays on a per-use basis. Key – Organization will have almost full control of assets placed within this model.

Inherent Risk For the purposes of this process inherent risk is defined as an application or system "devoid of controls" or "a raw risk that has no mitigation factors or treatments applied to it."

Integrity Integrity refers to being correct or consistent with the intended state of information. Any unauthorized modification of data, whether deliberate or accidental, is a breach of data integrity. For example, data stored on disk are expected to be stable – they are not supposed to be changed at random by problems with the disk controllers. Similarly, application programs are supposed to record information correctly and not introduce deviations from the intended values.

Parkerian Hexad This is a set of six elements of information security proposed by Donn B. Parker in 1998. The Parkerian hexad adds three additional attributes to the three classic security attributes of the CIA triad. These attributes of information are atomic in that they are not broken

---

[1] MITRE, Common Weakness Enumeration, 2020, https://cwe.mitre.org/about/index.html

down into further constituents; they are non-overlapping in that they refer to unique aspects of information. Any information security breach can be described as affecting one or more of these fundamental attributes of information.

Platform as a Service (PaaS) This is a category of cloud computing services that provides a computing platform and a solution stack as a service. In this model, the consumer creates the software using tools and/or libraries from the provider. The consumer also controls software deployment and configuration settings. The provider provides the networks, servers, storage, and other services that are required to host the consumer's application. Key – Organization will have some configuration, software, and provisioning choices. However, most of the operational aspects will be controlled by the provider.

Possession Possession or Control: Suppose a thief were to steal a sealed envelope containing a bank debit card and its personal identification number. Even if the thief did not open that envelope, it's reasonable for the victim to be concerned that the thief could do so at any time. That situation illustrates a loss of control or possession of information but does not involve the breach of confidentiality.

Risk Risk is a measure of the extent to which an entity is threatened by a potential circumstance or event, and is typically a function of (i) the adverse impacts that would arise if the circumstance or event occurs; and (ii) the likelihood of occurrence.

Risk Appetite The level of risk that an organization is prepared to accept before action is deemed necessary to reduce it. It represents a balance between the potential benefits of innovation and the threats that change inevitably brings. The appropriate level will depend on the nature of the work undertaken and the objectives pursued. For example, where public safety is critical (e.g. operating a nuclear power station) appetite will tend to be low while for an innovative project (e.g. early development of an innovative computer program) it may be very high, with the acceptance of short-term failure that could pave the way to longer term success. Below are examples of broad approaches to setting risk appetite that a business may adopt to ensure a response to risk that is proportionate given their business objectives:

Averse Avoidance of risk and uncertainty is a key organization objective.

Minimal Preference for ultra-safe options that are low risk and only have a potential for limited reward.

Cautious   Preference for safe options that have a low degree of risk and may only have limited potential for reward.

Open   Willing to consider all potential options and choose the one most likely to result in successful delivery while also providing an acceptable level of reward and value for money.

Hungry   Eager to be innovative and to choose options offering potentially higher business rewards, despite greater inherent risk.

The appropriate approach may vary across an organization, with different parts of the business adopting an appetite that reflects their specific role, with an overarching risk appetite framework to ensure consistency.

Residual Risk   This is commonly defined as "the level of risk remaining after the relevant controls have been applied."

Risk Assessment   Risk assessment is the process of identifying, estimating, and prioritizing information security risks. Assessing risk requires the careful analysis of threat and vulnerability information to determine the extent to which circumstances or events could adversely impact an organization and the likelihood that such circumstances or events will occur.

Risk Assessment Methodology   A risk assessment methodology typically includes (i) a risk assessment process; (ii) an explicit risk model, defining key terms and assessable risk factors and the relationships among the factors; (iii) an assessment approach (e.g., quantitative, qualitative, or semi-qualitative), specifying the range of values those risk factors can assume during the risk assessment and how combinations of risk factors are identified/analyzed so that values of those factors can be functionally combined to evaluate risk; and (iv) an analysis approach (e.g. threat-oriented, asset/impact-oriented, or vulnerability-oriented), describing how combinations of risk factors are identified/analyzed to ensure adequate coverage of the problem space at a consistent level of detail.

Software as a Service (SaaS)   Sometimes referred to as "on-demand software" supplied by independent software vendors (ISVs) or "application service providers" (ASPs), SaaS is a software delivery model in which software and associated data are centrally hosted on the cloud. SaaS is typically accessed by users using a thin client via a web browser. Key – Organization does not maintain, administer, or provision access.

Threat   Anything that can exploit a vulnerability, intentionally or accidentally, and obtain, damage, or destroy an asset.

Utility   Utility means usefulness. For example, suppose someone encrypted data on disk to prevent unauthorized access or undetected modifications and then lost the decryption key – that would be a breach of utility. The data would be confidential, controlled, integral, authentic, and available – they just wouldn't be useful in that form. Similarly, conversion of salary data from one currency into an inappropriate currency would be a breach of utility, as would the storage of data in a format inappropriate for a specific computer architecture; e.g. EBCDIC instead of ASCII or 9-track magnetic tape instead of DVD-ROM. A tabular representation of data substituted for a graph could be described as a breach of utility if the substitution made it more difficult to interpret the data. Utility is often confused with availability because breaches such as those described in these examples may also require time to work around the change in data format or presentation. However, the concept of usefulness is distinct from that of availability.

Vulnerability   Weaknesses or gaps in a security program that can be exploited by threats to gain unauthorized access to an asset.

About the Author and Chapter Authors

 RICHARD O. MOORE III, MSIA, CISSP, CISM, AUTHOR AND EDITOR

Mr. Moore began his career developing the foundation of his operational and technical skills during his 15 years of military service with the U.S. Marine Corps Intelligence Community. He continued his passion for protecting information and creating sound cyber risk practices when he transitioned to the private sector as a consultant with KPMG providing security services for various public, private, and governmental institutions and subsequently assumed a senior leadership role with the Royal Bank of Scotland Americas, leading the institution's regulatory and data protection programs and building the cyber intelligence and cyber risk program.

Prior to creating CyberSix, Mr. Moore served as the Managing Director of Global Cyber Risk Services at Alvarez and Marsal and as the Chief Information Security Officer at New York Life Insurance Company. In these roles, he implemented an agile and transformational information security program that fostered an integrated "Intelligence and Risk" culture and program, providing executive management with a business-focused view of the company's cyber risks landscape. As part of the Intelligence and Risk program, he was accountable for leading and collaborating with a group of cross-functional executives in enhancing the company's overall cyber and operational risk management capabilities. He was responsible for leading complex technical and operational mitigation efforts associated with the company's threat landscape and regulatory matters.

Mr. Moore has served on numerous industry and client advisory boards and has been an Adjunct Professor at Salve Regina University and at Northeastern University Graduate Information Assurance programs. In addition to his university lectures, Mr. Moore is frequently a featured speaker at numerous industry conferences and a contributing author of information security books and articles. Mr. Moore earned a Masters in Information Assurance from Norwich University. Currently, he sits on two academic advisory boards and several advisory boards for cybersecurity technologies.

 ## STEVEN JOHNSON, DSC, CISM, CISSP, CCE #1463

Dr. Johnson is an industry veteran with over 15 years of experience in leading enterprise technology and information security programs. He holds a Doctor of Science degree in Cybersecurity with a concentration in risk management and strategy, and currently serves as Chief Technology Risk Officer at a top-tier investment bank based in New York City.

Previously, Dr. Johnson has held the roles of Chief Technology Information Security Risk Officer and Divisional Chief Information Security Officer at Fortune 100 and global financial institutions. A dedicated academic, Dr. Johnson is currently serving as an adjunct faculty member at Roger Williams University, providing instruction in forensics, malware analysis, intrusion detection, IT audit, and governance.

Early in his career, Dr. Johnson attained the Certified Computer Examiner (CCE) certification solidifying his expertise in digital forensics. When not mentoring and teaching aspiring cybersecurity professionals, Dr. Johnson can be found in the paddocks of North America's most iconic racetracks as an avid sports car endurance racer.

 ## DEREK OLSON, CISSP, CISM

Mr. Olson began his career in cybersecurity over 20 years ago when he transitioned from systems administration and network engineering to security, melding his love of technology and passion for security. In his 20 years, he has held roles in security operations and governance, risk, and compliance for Fortune 500 companies.

Mr. Olson participates in numerous information security organizations, such as ISC2 and ISACA. With over 17 years of information security experience, Mr. Olson has had the opportunity speak at ISACA membership conferences in Latin America as well as to the Panamanian Bankers Association (Association Bancaria de Panamá).

Mr. Olson holds a Master of Science degree in Information Assurance and Security as well as a Bachelor of Science degree in Information Systems and Technology Management with a focus on Information Security, from Capella University located in Minneapolis, Minnesota. Mr. Olson has received multiple industry-recognized credentials, including the Certified Information Systems Security Professional (CISSP), Certified Information Security Manager (CISM), GIAC Certified Incident Handler (GCIH), and GIAC Systems and Network Auditor (GSNA).

STEVEN M DUFOUR, ISO LEADER AUDITOR, CERTIFIED QUALITY MANAGER

Mr. Dufour is a US Army Veteran and an accomplished global IT Services executive with more than 30 years of experience in international executive management consulting, information technology, technology transfer and outsourcing. Mr. Dufour has developed and launched over 5 successful international startups serving Government and Commercial markets in the area of C5ISR, Machine Learning & Artificial Intelligence, Advanced Analytics and Cyber Security.

Mr. Dufour has held the roles of Chief Development Officer, Chief Technology Officer, Chief Information Officer, Chief Operating Officer and Chief Executive Officer. Across all of these roles, Mr. Dufour has successfully led large-scale, complex, global service operations involving operational transformation, technology transfer, global delivery and expansion, merger acquisition and integration, and the management and development of international client engagements. Mr. Dufour has provided value-added services to several large multinationals to include; Caterpillar Tractor, Altria Group, Philip Morris, John Deere, Toro Manufacturing, Roche Pharmaceutical, Proctor & Gamble, Raytheon, Detroit Diesel and General Motors.

Steve has a Bachelor of Science degree in Information Technology Management and has expanded his formal education with advanced studies in the areas of International Business Management, Mergers and Acquisitions, Information Technology and Global Program Management. Mr. Dufour has attended international business management programs at the London School of Business, Kellogg Executive Development at Northwestern University and the Executive Development Program at the Foster College of Business.

Index